I followed my Bliss
to Bankruptcy

What
I Wish
I KNEW™

before I Moved
to Hollywood

I followed my Bliss
to Bankruptcy

What
I Wish
I KNEW™

before I Moved
to Hollywood

T. R. LOCKE

Cover design and layout by: Jana Rade, impact studios
Edited by: Jill Rembar

Published by Wish I Knew® Books
A Division of Media City Publishers
1020 N. Hollywood Way, Suite 108
Burbank, CA 91505

Visit T.R. Locke on myspace at: www.myspace.com/trlocke
Or on Facebook at: www.trlocke.go2fb.com

Printed in the United States of America

First Edition: December 2008
10 9 8 7 6 5 4 3 2 1

LIBRARY OF CONGRESS CATALOGING-IN-PUBLICATION DATA
has been applied for.

ISBN: 978-0-9818983-0-8

Attention: Schools and Corporations
Wish I Knew® Books are available at quantity discounts with bulk purchase for educational, business, or sales promotional use. For information, please write to Special Sales Department, Wish I Knew Books, 1020 N. Hollywood Way, Suite 108, Burbank, CA 91505. Or call Media City at 818-581-2118.

For Lisa, for saving me, for believing in me and for loving me throughout our journey thus far...

For Aja, for letting Daddy write after only minimal play time and making our lives so much fun.

For Mom, for believing in me and reminding me that if all else fails, I could always become as a short-order cook.

Contents

Introduction:
The Backside of Mount Hollywood

From where I sit writing this, in a converted garden shed in my backyard in Burbank, California, I can see the backside of Mount Hollywood. People familiar with Los Angeles know that behind the most famous mountain in the world sits the San Fernando Valley. Beyond that are more mountains and valleys, the Mojave Desert, and eventually Las Vegas.

For those of us who live in The Valley, as it's called, we rarely see the famous face of that mountain where "HOLLYWOOD" is sprawled out in giant white letters. And yet, half of the studios—Warner Bros., Disney, NBC, ABC, the WB network, and Universal are back here with us. Sony (Columbia) is all the way down in Culver City near LAX and Fox is over in Century City near Beverly Hills. In fact, the only major studio in Hollywood is Paramount, and it is also the only one with a view of the Hollywood sign.

I think the fact that most of the folk in the industry don't see that sign is a good metaphor. Most people in the world understand Hollywood from the perspective of the front of that sign—the searchlight glamour, the glory, the magic. This book is about what's behind that sign—the backside most folk in the industry see every day, but the side people outside the industry never see.

This book is about the real world that hundreds of thousands of writers, actors, filmmakers, comedians, singers, dancers, models, producers, makeup artists, editors, and other dreamers experience each morning in the real Hollywood.

Back here it's not as glamorous or exciting, but it is intriguing. Most superstars have lived at least some of this life before they made it, so it is part of their story, too—the part left on the cutting room floor.

Either way, I can say this book holds what I wish I knew before I moved here. Call it a prospectus or a market analysis to review before you or your loved one invests. And if you have no Hollywood dreams, enjoy it with the type of detached curiosity you might have when visiting a strange new zoo. Hopefully, the antics of the creatures herein will keep you entertained.

Or... consider other dreams you may have—ones you may be thinking of pursuing but perhaps haven't begun to go after yet—the business you want to start, the Peace Corps service you want to experience, the property you want to buy, the child you want to adopt. Dreamers, aspirants, and yearners – these are the people for whom I've written this book. People who, in some way, sense there is a more interesting road to travel. People who find the idea of trying something completely new and different both terrorizing and tantalizing. People who know in their gut that one day they will. They will buy that motorcycle. They will parachute from 30,000 feet. They will become a millionaire. This book is for dreamers and those who know and love them.

You don't know me—not yet. But my original impulse to write this book came from an experience I had in a meeting with a production company (prodco), the details of which I shared with a screenwriters group I attend. The group members suggested I share that story and others like it with you. It's a cautionary tale that you may find has a lot of resonance with your world.

A few years ago I read books by two of Hollywood's most famous screenwriters: William Goldman's *Adventures in the Screen Trade*, and a memoir by Joe Eszterhas—*Hollywood Animal*.

Goldman weaves his stories of firsthand encounters with classic movie stars like Robert Redford and Dustin Hoffman with charm and wit and a hint of cynicism.

Eszterhas, famous in Hollywood for his madman temper (after he allegedly pulled a knife at a meeting with his agent), and for penning some of the most expensive scripts ever sold, notably *Flashdance* and *Basic Instinct*, writes scathing criticism of the Hollywood machine and his bouts with drugs, alcohol, debauchery and movie stars to help himself cope.

After reading their books, I realized that although I had stories of life in Hollywood, none of them involved gratitude sex from Sharon Stone for making her a star, as Eszterhas had claimed. Nor had any of my stories involved me measuring my height against Sylvester Stallone's in some swimming pool in Cannes, France, as Goldman did. I had pulled no knives on powerful agents, nor gone on Hemingway-like rum and cocaine binges. None of my stories included million-dollar paychecks (let alone the $30M Eszterhas has allegedly made from his scripts) because I had yet to sell anything.

I had, however, met a few successful people, a ton of wannabes and pretenders, and more people on their way down than I even imagined existed.

I'd seen stars at amusement parks with their families, in grocery stores, in Home Depot, at some event I'd gotten invited to, or driving behind me on the Ventura Freeway, but never in any real meetings.

Sure I could reach out and touch them (if I wanted to get arrested), but it was almost as if they lived on the other side of a mirror. I could see them, and yet speaking, smiling, or nodding to them was just as likely ignored as met with a response in kind. To them I didn't really exist. I was a nobody, so getting them to read my script so they would ultimately make my movie? That involved penetrating the actor's force field—their agent, who first applied his decontaminate and safety tests before that star, only two feet away from me, would ever read my script.

Unfortunately, the first decontamination test the agents applied was called "Cash Attached," which my scripts always failed—I'll explain why later.

Nonetheless, I did have a Hollywood story, just not one played out in front of the sign under blazing searchlights. Mine took place behind the sign—in the shadows cast by those giant white letters.

My story is valid and just as absurd as the ones you see on TV. People said they couldn't wait to read my Hollywood Insider Memoir. They assumed I'd write it after I'd had gratitude sex with Sharon Stone (or to update it a bit, Gabrielle Union) and after I'd gotten that million-dollar check, abused drugs and thrown up in the grotto at the Playboy Mansion.

Screw that. Who knows if Hollywood would ever appreciate my writing? In essence, my fellow writers and I were doing just what we complained Hollywood did—we were waiting on me to succeed before believing anyone would care about what I had to say.

So at that point it hit me. If I waited until I was a successful screenwriter, my book wouldn't be much different from Goldman's or Eszterhas'. But even more importantly, if I waited, I would forget the irritation, disillusionment and pain that motivate me now. I would happily forget about the players that lied to me and, in essence, the very soul of this book would be lost to time.

After all, that's what happens with success—you forget the pain because you're too busy going to parties with the same assholes who crapped on you before. But right now, right here, I'm in the midst of my struggle.

Three years ago my manager called and told me he was getting out of the movie production and management business to be dean of external development for Loyola Marymount Film School.

"Loyola Marymount? But you're Jewish!" I reminded him.

"I've got two kids in college and I need to watch out for the future. I'm sorry. I'll still do everything I can to help you out."

"Can you refer me to another manager?"

"Sure."

He didn't. We chatted a few times off and on, mostly e-mails, a lunch or two. No referrals until it was too late. But that story comes later, too.

See, if I waited until I "succeeded" to write this, he'd be back in the business, ready to produce my next script, and reminding me how he was the first one to believe in me and try to seriously get my film made. I would have to admit he was right. Somehow I would have linked my success to his initial encouragement and maybe even given him credit for leaving me, which, no doubt, led to my pushing open doors myself, which I'd have never done if he had stayed. We'd be friends again and I could never talk about him like I can now.

Not only did my manager quit, but shortly afterwards, I fired my agent. Let me write that again. Not only did my manager quit, but shortly afterwards, I fired my agent.

I wrote that line twice because I didn't believe it myself the first time. It's unusual for a writer who hasn't sold to even land an agent. In fact, there are plenty of writers who *have* sold something who can't even get an agent. To fire one is an act of self-destruction tantamount to crack abuse.

After I fired my agent, I spent some time in depression, and I just stopped writing anything except journal entries. Then I shifted gears to take advantage of the booming L.A. real estate market.

That is until recently, when the L.A. real estate market tanked and a producer, who happened to read something I had written in an e-mail to some friends, called and told me I was an amazing writer and I should turn that particular e-mail into a script. I'm in the process of negotiating the contract on that script now. Amazing.

So, after months of depression, and now a couple more years of experiences, I'm ready to write about agents, managers, producers, directors, and all the other insanity I've encountered on my journey here in Hollywood.

In thinking about the structure of this book, I figured I should explore how the hell I got here in the first place. So, with that, a third catalyst to write this book kicked in: What made me think I could make it as a Hollywood screenwriter? What did I think Hollywood was about? And would I have sold my stuff and moved here had I known then what I know now?

My personal answer is "hell no!" But that's because of what I had to deal with naively, and the pain it brought into my life. Had I known beforehand to expect it, maybe it wouldn't have hurt so badly, or at least I would have been better prepared. That's my hope for you as you read this.

My answer is moot because I didn't know. I didn't have the advantage of someone giving me the inside "really real" on what's up out here.

The way I see it, the picture people get of Hollywood is way too distorted to understand clearly. Maybe the fact that our culture is celebrity and money-obsessed makes the lure of this city irresistible.

Or maybe writers, actors, and other artists like myself see movies, think they are so cool, and just want to be part of that world without having any clear notion of what that world—the real one, not the movie or TV version—looks like, feels like, or is.

And maybe the reason we don't know is because cameras only follow the stars and the ones who have succeeded and who live the dream.

That's what all the other books have been about—that's what we're drawn to—the spotlight side of Hollywood. But to get to that side, most come this way, the way I came—through dark shadows, without a map. Let this book be that map.

By the way, I'm not some guy fresh off the bus. I do have some success. I still have two agents—a theatrical acting agent and a commercial acting agent. I've booked national commercials and TV shows and I've had money—real money—offered for my scripts. Yet this "success" hasn't been enough to make a living by itself. Not in California. Not even close. This new deal I'm negotiating now may change all that, but it hasn't yet.

So read on. Maybe you save yourself or a loved one some serious pain. Or maybe you figure out a better way to make it, or some shortcut. Or you polish your stuff in your hometown and e-mail it to Hollywood instead of moving here. That way you don't stand too close to the vampire that lives by sucking the life-blood from your creative heart.

There's crazy crap in these pages. Better on these pages than on a plate set before you to eat. Here's what I wish I knew before I came here—the benign and the terrifying.

Before we get to that though, this next chapter looks at why I became a writer and what made me think I could make it in Hollywood. It's important because it looks at what factors in life and personality can combine to make a person give up the safe path to pursue something risky. Admittedly, that part will be more memoir than help—although I believe people who pursue dreams in Hollywood share similar traits. Nonetheless, if you just want to know what things you'd better know before you come to Hollywood, you can skip the next few pages and get right to the chapter titled "Welcome to Hollywood" and the chapters I call "WIKs," for the things I "Wish I Knew."

Finally, through the years of living here, I've come to know quite a few people who've made successful careers. The fourth and final catalyst for writing this book was a desire to know what those who've already succeeded experienced behind the Hollywood sign. That section of this book is entitled "What They Wish They Knew." For your edification, there are my interviews with real Hollywood players, including successful writers, producers, award-winning actors, comedians, makeup artists, Grammy nominated singers, hip-hop producers, TV stars, and more. Take advantage of the advice they have to offer to someone looking to make it in Hollywood. What they share may stun you, but their insights are invaluable in understanding the world as it works here.

I hope this book helps you or someone you love shortcut past years of emotional and financial pain on the road to your bliss. If not, perhaps you'll at least get some laughs out of it. –TRL

Part I:
Dreams

"A dream can be nurtured over years and years and then flourish rapidly. Be patient. It will happen for you. Sooner or later, life will get weary of beating on you and holding the door shut on you, and then it will let you in and throw you a real party."
—Les Brown

"Don't ask so much what the world needs. Go out and do what makes you come alive, because what the world needs most are people who have come alive."
—Howard Thurman

"He felt his whole life was some kind of dream and he sometimes wondered whose it was and whether they were enjoying it."
—Douglas Adams

What Was I Thinking?

Ahh, dreams. Without them, what kind of world would this be?

A rtists can usually recall the event or the turning point that led them to the creative path. Most likely it occurred in school. For me, it was in sixth grade. My sister Cherry took me to work with her. I'd never seen a computer before. The whole time, I sat before the screen amazed. The Qwerty keyboard was a confusing mess, but she didn't even have to look at it. She typed so fast that her fingers blurred, yet she made words appear out of nothing on the green monochrome monitor. Like some secret code transmission, it was the coolest thing I'd ever seen. I had to learn to do that.

I imagine that I am the only boy in the world who asked his dad to buy him a typewriter for a sixth grade graduation present. A typewriter? Off to Sears we went.

Dad was a Sears man. Mom was a JCPenney woman. The two stores were at opposite ends of the biggest mall in the world at that time—Randall Park Mall, just outside Cleveland. "Owned and Operated by Edward J. DeBartolo." People in our neighborhood said DeBartolo was a mobster. He owned all the malls. And he owned the racetrack across the street from the mall. In fact, I think he owned the entire city of North Randall. On Saturday evenings, a private plane would land at the track and haul the cash he raked in off to Youngstown, where he lived. I remember he later bought the San Francisco 49ers for his son as a birthday present. I don't know if he was in the mob, or if he was just a successful Italian businessman, but buying your son a professional football team for his birthday is pretty "gangster." But I digress...

I got my typewriter and started teaching myself to type that summer. When school started back, I found myself hopping a bus to the ghetto to attend Alexander Hamilton Junior High Major Work Magnet School.

"Major Work" was what later got termed college prep or advanced placement—smart kids' school. But I hated it and was willing to give up the better education for a safer, more esthetically pleasing environment in my own neighborhood. So mom had me transferred to Charles Elliot—walking distance from my house.

I don't know if it was because I was new to the school or if I just figured I needed something to do with my new typewriter, or if I was just a huge liar, but for some reason, I started telling huge lies. I'm sorry... HUGE LIES. I should put a reference note here and in the back of the book have a whole page with giant type just saying "HUGE" and another page saying "LIES."

There was a TV show on at the time called "Real People." During the credits, the name of the assistant director scrolled up: "Rick Locke." The last name Locke is rare enough, so it caught my eye. It was the first time I'd ever seen anyone else, outside my family, with my last name. (I was in high school before I ever heard the name John Locke.)

Some kid asked me where my dad worked. For some reason, I said he was the assistant director for "Real People." The kid didn't believe me until I told him to check the credits at the end of the show. His reaction the day after checking the credits was near worship. I guess it started there.

As the rumor spread, different kids would question me. I kept the lie going.

My sister had done some modeling a few years earlier, so when anyone asked, I said my sister was a model. She really worked for the municipal gas company, in customer service.

My other sister had just graduated from college and wanted to be a lawyer. She had yet to enroll in or even apply for law school (in fact, she never did), but when they asked, I told them she was a successful lawyer.

It became a game to see how big and outrageous a lie I could tell. I made my whole family something akin to the Ewings on *Dallas* or the Carringtons on *Dynasty*. Or maybe we were more like the Tates on *Soap*.

My brother lived in Oklahoma and worked on an oil rig, so it made sense to me to say that he owned an oil company.

My mom had worked at a drapery store, so I'm not sure how I came to cast her as DeBartolo's executive secretary, but I did. And my dad, a near-retired steelworker and shop steward for 40 years at Republic Steel in Cleveland—well, I made him an assistant TV director in Hollywood, which was the same as a movie director to my seventh-grade mind.

The main question I would get was why I lived in Cleveland and went to a public school. "Well, Dad and Mom were divorced and he's too busy to raise me and ... blah, blah, blah... but I get to see him once a month when he flies me out to Hollywood." And that seemed to suffice. Because, after all, "I don't like to talk about it."

I suppose to help quiet doubts I decided to type a letter on my new typewriter. The letter was from "J.W. Paramount," who, in that same seventh-grade mind, was the most believable name for the owner of Paramount Studios.

The letter said that they were going to be shooting a movie in Cleveland, which my dad would be directing. It also said that they wanted me to audition talent at the school on the studio's behalf.

My best friend Cedrick watched me type it and kept my secret. But the official-looking signature came from my mom. Mom's always been a bit crazy. She signed it in big, flowing, grown-up, cursive letters—
J.W. Paramount. And off I went to school, letter in hand, to show the doubters.

I didn't anticipate Valerie. She grabbed my letter and took it to our math teacher. The math teacher pulled me out of class and asked, "Is this for real?"

It was too late to back down. "Yes. It's real." And off we went to the English teacher. She asked the same question. I gave the same answer. And off we went to the principal's office—all three of us, down the red tile hall—my proverbial road to Oz.

The principal asked the same question. I gave the same answer—completely poker-faced.

Looking back on it as an adult, this situation makes no sense to me. I have no idea what they really believed because there couldn't have been an address or phone number on the letter—I doubt I thought of that, and they certainly didn't call anyone. It wasn't computer generated, it was typewriter typed. There was no pre-printed letterhead, just onion-skinned typing paper titled, "From the Desk of J.W. Paramount" across the top and addressed "To Whom It May Concern."

I don't recall my spelling and grammar being good, but it must have been convincing—either that, or they were so caught up in the fantasy that they didn't bother thinking it through. Or maybe they were trying to set me up to teach me a lesson.

Whatever the case, the principal said, "Wow, this is so cool," and had the English teacher schedule auditions. An announcement came over the loudspeaker and my first script was greenlighted for production.

I became an instant celebrity. The English teacher, Mrs. Talbert, ran the auditions with utmost seriousness. Cedrick and I sat in a corner taking notes "for my dad" with a clipboard. Both of us fully invested in our roles.

Kids followed me and Cedrick home, begging for a part. "I can't promise anything. My dad has the final say. I've got your number. Don't call me, I'll call you." I was a natural. All the makings of a Hollywood player and I was only twelve.

I still remember one boy's fervent plea, "I'll do anything to be in that movie," he said. I've learned a lot of people will. And they're often the ones who make it.

All my life I've tried to understand what happened next, why it happened precisely at that time, and what would have happened if circumstances had unfolded differently. Teachers went on strike all over Cleveland. They went on strike for more than three months. We returned to school in the middle of winter. But I never returned to Charles Elliot.

Chief Judge Frank Battisti had ruled the schools were unfairly segregated and that they must be desegregated. Busing had come to Cleveland. Everyone from Elliot now went to Jamison—another ugly neighborhood as far as I was concerned.

But the major work magnet junior high school was now in the beautiful new Whitney Young Junior High School building, in an even nicer area than Elliot. I was given an opportunity to escape the dilemma of my own creation, and I took it. Gladly. Thank God.

And since then, I've always either gotten in trouble, or gotten praised, or at the very least, gotten lots of attention for my writing.

At Whitney Young I wrote an essay for a scholarship competition. The essay's question was, "Who is Whitney Young?" My response argued that although our school was named for him, and I passed his picture in the hallway every day and thus knew he was a black man, apparently the school didn't think him important enough for students to study in the curriculum or else they wouldn't have to ask that question as part of a scholarship contest.

After that essay had circulated among the faculty and administration, I found myself an honorary student council member. My English teacher said that the essay was passed to the school board and when they read it, "the shit hit the fan." I understand that shortly thereafter, the school instituted a black history curriculum.

I didn't have to deal with the consequences of my lies about the movie for three years, but at John Marshall high school, I rejoined some of the kids from Elliot. That's when Latonya Dutton cornered me outside of Mrs. Wilson's math class. "Whatever happened to that movie your dad was directing?" she said with a look of *I'm older now; you can't fool me with your stupid lies.*

I actually remembered Latonya's audition. She had given a particularly good reading, plus she was cute. I had placed a star next to her name on my clipboard three years before. I would have definitely cast her if the movie had been real.

Luckily, I'd had three years to prepare for this day. "They decided to film it in New York and set it in an arts high school. It became the movie *Fame*. Did you see it?"

Latonya stared at me. I stared back. She stared some more. If it had been a poker game, she would have called me. "It was a good movie. You should see it. Sorry, but my dad got replaced on the project." I then walked away quickly—very quickly. And when anyone else from my past asked about it, I simply mentioned the *Fame* story and said I was angry I didn't get a part and "I don't want to talk about it."

In that tenth grade year, I became a comedy columnist with the school newspaper. At the end of that year, I won a scholarship to Wooster College for a summer writing camp. I started keeping a journal there, which I still do, to this day—nearly 25 years later.

In my senior year, I became the school paper's editor-in-chief and received a special citywide award for Best High School Newspaper.

In college, I was praised for my writing, won a couple scholarships, and got entered in creative writing contests by my Literature and Writing professors. The chairman of the English department even took me to lunch one day to tell me I had a gift and should pursue it.

I didn't pursue writing, though. I had come to college with a different purpose... Ministry.

I had what I was told was "a calling on my life." Like some drug-addicted college kid who is transformed after he gets a letter from the Dalai Lama informing him he is the reincarnated soul of a great ancient warrior and needs to report to training, my pastor told me the reason I didn't like any of my jobs out of high school was because I was supposed to be in ministry.

How I came to have a pastor is an interesting story. Especially since I'd never stepped foot inside a church until I was fifteen. At fifteen, I went to church with the secret goal of learning how I might become the Antichrist.

Let me back up a second. If you'd asked me when I was in junior high school what I wanted to do with my life, and I'd answered honestly, I would have said I wanted to be the Antichrist. I got that idea from a movie, *Damien Omen II*. I imagine that that movie had the same kind of effect on me that *Harry Potter* or *X-Men* might have on some young boys today. I wanted to be able to control people with my mind. I wanted power and I wanted it bad. And Damien had power. And he was so cool with it.

I loved that movie so much that I bought the book. In one scene, Damien's cousin gets picked on at the military school they attend. When the bully won't stop, Damien just stares at him and the boy starts screaming in pain until blood drips from his nose and... he dies! Wild! According to the book, the boy's brain twisted inside his head! Yeah! I wanted that!

The thing about *Damien Omen II* that's different from *X-Men* and

Harry Potter is that it deals with stuff from the Bible that millions of people believe to be true. In the movie, Damien reads from the Book of Revelation and discovers he has a 666 birthmark under his hairline. I searched for days for those sixes—all up in the mirror with my mom's compact—hoping to find the mark of the beast. I went and found a Bible in the house and started reading the Book of Revelation to see what else I could learn. Maybe the mark could be hiding in other places.

While I was reading, my mom came home and asked what I was doing. Then she informed me that her church Bible study had just started on the Book of Revelation and I could go there and learn more. I showed up there the next week.

I was scared out of my mind after studying Revelation and reading a book by Hal Lindsay entitled *The Late Great Planet Earth* and I was convinced the end of the world was nigh. Next thing I knew, I was getting baptized and joining a church. I decided to join the good side because things didn't end too well for the Antichrist.

Meanwhile, in addition to writing for the high school newspaper, I was an actor in school plays and a radio announcer in the mornings. I became so convinced that Jesus was going to sneak up on everyone I knew, that I had to warn them. So one morning, without permission or notice, I started reading the Bible over the school radio and put the whole school in the same state of panicked paranoia I lived in inside my head.

As I read, my hands could barely hold steady the paper I'd typed. I was terrified. And by the time the advisor cut me off and the vice-principals and security guards stormed the radio room, everyone else in my school was terrified too.

I don't know what all the fallout of that crazy stunt was, but one thing that happened was that I was branded a preacher. So, when I graduated, everyone assumed I'd go to college to study ministry—everyone but me.

I had no intention of going to college because in my senior year of high school Billy Graham came out with a book entitled, *Approaching*

Hoofbeats, The Four Horsemen of the Apocalypse. After reading the book by the world's most famous evangelist, which reinforced what I'd read in *The Late Great Planet Earth*, I began to believe that Jesus was due to return in 1987—only two years away—so I wouldn't have time to finish college anyway.[1]

In 1988, three years and ten unsatisfying jobs later, I was selling insurance and bored out of my skull. Jesus hadn't come back and I hadn't really prepared for the possibility that he wouldn't. I was actually disappointed rather than relieved because I gave up a lot of my youth worrying that I'd get caught by Jesus doing something I shouldn't be doing instead of just living my life.

I went to see my pastor about it. He told me the rapture would take care of itself and that he believed I was avoiding a calling on my life. He then said that I wouldn't be happy until I became what God wanted me to be. He told me God wanted me to go to college. He even told me the school I should go to—a specific Christian college in Chicago. So at twenty-one, off I went.

At that college, I was required to do a weekly community service. I got assigned to serve at the Cook County Detention center—the largest youth detention center in the country. Every kid I met there was involved in one gang or another. By the end of my freshman year I had a job working with street gangs and I lived in Humboldt Park, on the corner of Whipple and Wabansia, in the heart of the "Almighty Latin Kings Nation."

Just prior to my moving there, Humboldt Park had been honored with the title *Most Gang-Infested Neighborhood in the USA.* It also picked up a small award for being the *Neighborhood with the Most Homicides Per Capita in the USA.* That didn't stop me from jogging through its beautiful two square mile city park every morning, and cooling off with a skinny-dip in the swimming beach afterwards. No one was ever there in the mornings. Nights were a different thing.

---

1   *The end of 1987 was the end of one generation (40 years) after the refounding of the state of Israel. Lindsay argued that was when the "rapture" of the church would occur. His book sold over 15 million copies at that time.*

Kids showed up at my door at 2 a.m. with bleeding bullet wounds, begging me to hide them. Gunshots fired off all hours of the day and night, gang shorties washed my car for me in the open fire hydrant, and they helped me bring in groceries between their drug sales.

I became an unofficial member of about five gangs—Latin Kings, Gangster Disciples, Four Corner Hustlers, Imperial Gangsters, and Insane Vice Lords.

In my mind, at the time, that was where I belonged. I may have been encouraged to write, but I could think of doing nothing but more gang work when I graduated. However, part of that job, which I had throughout college and for four years afterwards, depended on my crafting fundraising letters, so I could reasonably say I did make my living from writing. Despite my "calling," I always believed I would eventually become a professional writer.

I got married at twenty-four, and moved my beautiful middle-class wife into the ghetto with me. Just before I turned twenty-six, I started to burn out on the gang work. We bought our first home so far outside the city that we had to drive past horses and cornfields on the way downtown every day.

Wifey worked for the *Chicago Sun-Times* and I took a new position at my alma mater, counseling college students instead of gang members. It was a pleasant change—regular working hours, a private office, a great view of the Chicago skyline outside my window, and no more 2 a.m. emergency phone calls.

But about three years later, something happened to change things. My daughter had been born, I'd written a couple magazine articles and book chapters based on my gang work, and I was feeling a bit antsy. Like the last time I'd gone to see my pastor, I was bored in my job. But I was doing ministry, so I figured that couldn't really be it. What was it then?

The Dave Matthews Band had just come out. I was listening to the radio on my way to work when I heard their first hit, *Ants Marching*. The Dan Ryan Expressway was jammed all the way into the Loop (downtown).

Next to me, people packed into the el train like mackerel at the 95th Street station. Commuters, cars, buses, trucks trudged across the bridge above my head and the words of the song captured it perfectly:

> *People in every direction*
> *No words exchanged*
> *No time to exchange them*
> *When all the little ants are marching*
> *Red and black antennae waving*
> *They all do it the same*
> *They all do it the same way*[2]

I felt antsy because I'd become an ant. I was marching along mindlessly—one hour each way, each day, every day, like everyone else. Chicago is topographically flat. I could see a straight line of cars for more than ten miles going into the anthill. Behind me another mile of cars were still coming on. And we looked just like ants marching. Only I had no idea what the point of it all was.

I suddenly swerved to avoid a chuckhole I knew I was about to hit. I knew it was there instinctively—not because I saw someone else swerve, but just because I knew that road that well and must have hit it a hundred times before. Its presence had become part of my subconscious. I had memorized that road so precisely that it no longer required conscious thought to navigate it, and that reality scared me. I became aware that, for years, I'd driven in and out of downtown Chicago in a mental haze—often arriving at home or work and not remembering the drive at all.

I decided right then it was time to become the writer I knew was inside of me. As the idea percolated over time, because I only wanted to write original stories, and didn't want to worry about them having

---

2   *"Ants Marching", Dave Matthews Band. © Bama Rags, Inc. and reproduced with permission. All rights reserved.*

to sell, I decided I'd make that possible by first becoming financially independent.

I worked hard investing for the next five years, eventually buying, rehabbing and renting out thirty-two apartment units in Chicago. The crap I went through in those five years merits a book of its own, *What I Wish I Knew Before I Invested in Real Estate*. (It's actually in the works.)

Anyway, I took the money I made and put it in the 2000 tech stock market. I had missed 300% growth from September 1999 to January 2000 because I was afraid the market would crash at the turn of the millennium—the dreaded "Y2K." The market didn't crash when it was supposed to. But three months later, after I put all my money firmly in tech funds... it did. I lost $300,000 and had nothing to show for that five years of work except the remaining equity in my buildings.

I got through that rough time with a combination of therapy and Oprah.

Oprah said something that interested me. I was frustrated that I'd worked so hard, sacrificed so much and still lost all that money. Oprah said, "*People don't find happiness when they chase money. Money can't be first. Instead, you should follow your bliss and the money will come.*"

Joseph Campbell coined the phrase "follow your bliss." The idea is basically that there is something at which each individual is naturally gifted and suited for success. An orange tree is suited to grow oranges and would not do well trying to grow pineapples, or raise chickens, or almost anything else for that matter.

People who are able to locate their natural giftedness and pursue their career in it will not only succeed financially but do so joyfully, as if not working at all.

Oprah argued at the time that many people, afraid of following their bliss because they didn't understand how to make money doing the things they loved, missed out on this concept and instead chased after financial security—anything to pay the bills. But in doing so they found themselves miserable.

Was that it? I hadn't been following my bliss? I was going after money first?

Will Smith had an album out at the time. In it, he had a line that said, "No plan B, it distracts from plan A." Is that what it was? I was following plan B of my life to get to plan A?

Oprah and Will couldn't be wrong, could they? Well, if success and apparent happiness were any indication of knowledge, they weren't. Maybe real estate wasn't my thing and I would and could only be happy once I started following my bliss.

Although I'd been primarily focused on writing books, at some point I read an article in *American Writer* magazine that posed the question, "Do you watch more movies than you read books?" My answer was yes. The article then suggested that perhaps I should be a screenwriter instead of an author. Hmmm. Flashbacks of junior high school and the movie world I'd briefly created flooded my mind.

I wrote my first script and entered it in a number of screenwriting contests. The first two, the Austin and the Chicago contests, rejected it. I then rewrote the script and sent it to the Chesterfield in L.A.

Spielberg's Amblin Entertainment had established the Chesterfield, so it was the big one to me. Not only was it in L.A. and affiliated with Stephen Spielberg, but the prize was a one-year writing fellowship in Hollywood and $25,000.

The other two contests awarded $5,000 and a trip to the host city. I was already living in Chicago and I imagined Austin was a nice place, but not as nice as L.A. I was ecstatic when my script went to the semi-finals of the Chesterfield.

I took a screenwriting class at Columbia College in Chicago. The teacher there loved my writing so much that he sent it to a Hollywood producer friend he'd met at a party at Roger Ebert's house. The producer also loved it and took it to another producer friend. Next thing I knew, they wanted to make my script and we were having two-hour phone conversations about which actors could play which roles. They wanted to send contracts to me in the mail. It was working. Following my bliss was paying off.

I wrote another script, which I thought was even better—an action script set on the moon that was just so damn cool. And I had ideas for five or six more.

So at the age of thirty-three, with an offer to purchase one script and an even better second script to sell, I packed up my family, sold my buildings, my home, my furniture (it was cheaper than moving it), and moved to Hollywood. I wanted to become a screenwriter. I was determined to follow my bliss.

Welcome to Hollywood, Baby!

There's something mystical about Los Angeles. I think it has to do with it seeming so familiar, even to people who've never been here.

So many movies and TV shows have been filmed against its mountainous background, palm trees, ocean beaches and streets that you just have this sense of *I know this place.* It puts you at ease very quickly.

Something else you'll notice here—people smile. People in L.A. smile far more than I've seen anywhere in the world, except Maui. Maybe they smile because so many in L.A. are actors hoping to be discovered and they never know who's looking. Or maybe it's the perpetual sunshine.

Or maybe it's because they have some of the whitest, brightest teeth on the planet. I've never seen such dental perfection. Teeth that make you stop and stare. Perfect teeth. Blazingly white, perfectly formed. My teeth weren't that white when they grew in. I don't know what they do here to get them that luminous, but it's impressive.

Whatever the reason, Angelenos smile and are very friendly. They smile. They speak. They start conversations. I'm not saying this is bad. For me it was just unexpected. I'm a friendly person, but I'm suspicious of over-friendly people. It took me a little while to get used to it. It took me a while to get used to a few more things, too.

I mention the sunshine because it never rains. Ever. Believe that. This is a desert. We arrived in August, and we did not see a drop of rain until November. It next rained in January, but not again until the following November. I never thought I'd miss rain. But if you've ever had weather play a major role in your day-to-day life, that will end in Los Angeles.

For me, rain often meant contemplation indoors. I can't think of many things more pleasing to me than to watch it rain outside while I'm safe indoors with a cup of coffee. No, there is one thing better—watching it snow outside and being indoors with a cup of coffee by a fireplace. But if I had to have just one weather experience every single day for months on end, I'd rather have sunshine. I guess that's true of many people because they pay a premium to live here.

If you decide to move here, first, obviously, you'll need a place to stay. There are lots of nice areas. If you've owned a home before, you'll probably imagine buying a similar one here. What you will soon find out is that the equivalent of your home, the one you were used to back where you came from, will be staggeringly expensive in L.A. That is, unless you're from New York, or unless the current market decline continues longer than expected. (Concerning the current market decline, our home's value, as of this writing, has dropped some $200,000. The sad part is that even if it dropped another $400,000, it would still be overpriced in my opinion.)

If you're lucky to be able to afford a home at all, it will be about a third the size you expect to have for the price. And for east coast and Midwest folk, say goodbye to basements and attics. Most likely you will settle into an apartment.

You may visit the ocean if you can find parking. It will look very familiar. That's because it's been filmed from every possible angle under the sun. What won't be familiar is when you go into the water and find it is ice cold. Not just cool—bone chilling. Even if it's 100 degrees on the sand (and it won't ever be that hot at the beach), the ocean will be frigid.

As a result of the cold ocean, when you travel from The Valley to the L.A. basin, you will find that temperatures drop ten to twenty degrees. If you end up settling in The Valley and it's 100 degrees outside (The Valley gets super hot in the summer), and you decide to go to the ocean, you will find that it is so much colder when you arrive at the ocean that you may forget why you wanted to go to the ocean in the first place.

In the wintertime, if you're in the city or west of the city, on a clear day, you will be able to look and see snow-covered mountains behind the downtown skyline. When it's 70 degrees outside, that's a weird sight, but it's also beautiful.

Another little point about the weather is that it's always cold as soon as the sun sets. You will learn very quickly to keep a jacket or sweatshirt in the car with you. (And *everyone* has a car. *No one* walks, or takes public transportation.) Once the sun goes down, temperatures drop twenty to thirty degrees minimum. Nights are always cold in L.A., even if it's eighty degrees in the daytime.

The only time L.A. has warm nights is when the Santa Ana winds blow. And when they blow, L.A. catches fire. Period. The already "worst polluted air in the country" will be thickened nicely with a generous dose of ash and smoke.

Although you may argue whether the air you see is fog or smog most days, you will have no doubt when it's orange.

I point out a few of these oddities because, in many ways, Hollywood itself is a bit mystical, surprising, confusing and toxic. Nonetheless, it is the center of the entertainment world. If you want to be in the entertainment business, it seems logical to be here.

So what do you need to know besides the fact that it never rains, that real estate is outrageously priced, that on 100 degree days you may still get frostbite in the ocean, that on seventy-degree days you can see snow-covered mountains and that, even though you can sometimes blow smoke rings with the air, everyone smiles perfect teeth at you?

Well, there are a few more things I Wish I Knew (WIK) before I moved here. Here they are...

Part II:
Realities

"But there is suffering in life, and there are defeats. No one can avoid them. But it's better to lose some of the battles in the struggles for your dreams than to be defeated without ever knowing what you're fighting for."
—Paulo Coelho

"I do my best work when I'm in pain and turmoil."
—Sting

"Thank you for the tragedy. I need it for my art."
—Kurt Cobain

The Competition Is
A Mother~#$&%!

You don't move to Hollywood because you think you have no talent. You move here because, like me, someone somewhere told you that you were good enough. You may even have had success, and good success, in your previous town. You've booked parts, made audiences roar with laughter, you've made them cry, and maybe even stand and applaud. Hold on to those memories, because none of that means anything here.

The dragon that is Hollywood eats and craps out one hundred times the equivalent of your entire creative career every single day, non-stop. Mike Myers' complete anthology would barely fill a single day of a single station's programming. I say this to illustrate the fact that there are tons of talented people here—the best and most talented in the entire world. How talented?

Well, law students from Harvard, Princeton, Yale, and every other Ivy League school work in the mailrooms of the agencies here just to get a foot in the door. The best and the brightest, who could work anywhere in the country, whore themselves out for pennies in Hollywood. But then they become the agents and managers, lawyers, and even producers that make all the deals.

That's not all though. How about Tyler Perry, who made $70M off his plays all over the country before he came to Hollywood to make a movie and then really blew up?

How about magicians who polish their acts before sold-out crowds on the Vegas Strip for years before daring to set foot in Hollywood?

How about singers who go platinum in their own hometowns before coming to Hollywood to "get to that next level?"

How about Jackie Chan, who made 100 movies in China before crossing the ocean to see what he could do here?

How about Simon Cowell and Nigel Lythgoe who produced *Next Great Pop Star* in England for years before coming to Hollywood to do *American Idol*?

John Grisham, Steven King, and J.K. Rowling can write million copy bestsellers, but can't write scripts. Meanwhile, David Koepp (*Jurassic Park, Spiderman,* and *Indiana Jones and the Kingdom of the Lost Skull*) gets $4M a script plus 2%. Some actors get paid $20M a movie here, plus a percentage. Some of them do two movies a year. Let's break that $40M down to a forty-hour per week salary. That's $769,230/week. $153,846/day. $19,230/hour. $321/min. $5/second.

At $240M/year, Oprah makes six times that amount. Just thought I'd throw that in because it's mind-blowing. So if you ever get a chance to talk to Oprah, know that her time is worth $32 a second, or $1,922/minute.

Of course they all work more than forty hours a week—so I guess it evens out. Yeah, right.

One of the actors whose interview appears later in this book earns $125,000/episode (basically, each week). He spoke to me for about an hour. At sixty hours a week (normal for network TV actors), the hour of time he gave me was worth $2,083.

But I say this so that you understand who your competition may be. Take a look at these people and their accomplishments and think about your level of commitment to the game. You may be talented, but you are certainly not alone in that department.

When you start to feel that something is hard, think about the competition and ask yourself, *What did I expect?*

Perhaps you play a sport. To draw a comparison, consider how much different a professional athlete's life is from yours. Day-in and day-out they condition, train, and focus—forcing their muscles to memorize the actions necessary to succeed in their sport.

If you play a decent game of basketball on weekends at the Y, you may want to think twice about your fitness for the NBA. Do you have that kind of commitment and focus? Do you have that level of desire? Is your game that tight? If not, you might want to stick with the Y on Saturdays.

When you step onto a film set and see Mark Wahlberg rehearsing his lines, or when you step into a conference room and see Phil Rosenthal trying to work out a joke, it's no different than stepping onto a basketball court and seeing LeBron James warming up. If Roger Federer is about to serve to you, you might want to know what you're doing.

You hear of kids drafted to the NBA out of high school, like Kevin Garnett. There's no doubt at all that such talent will generally prosper.

Will Smith was a successful young rapper from Philly who had made a name for himself rhyming about teenage issues and silliness. The creator of *Fresh Prince of Bel Air* saw his music video and brought him from Philly to L.A. specifically to star in that show. An audition was basically unnecessary. They just needed to see if he could say lines. Will never had to go to a ton of auditions, face rejection, try again, get rejected. Not in Hollywood anyway— though maybe in his music quests. He never saw this world here the way most have seen it. He was ushered in off his success in his hometown to a custom-made TV show, where he was allowed to develop his acting chops while being paid as an actor. The rest is history.

For those of us who've not been "discovered" and given free passage, or who have been brought here by producers or agents whose promises far outweighed their power, know that your competition includes the best and the brightest. It's exciting to be in a new place, and L.A. has a lot to distract you from your course, but don't forget to bring your A game or you'll find the ball and the game have moved past you before you know it.

Don't Worry; They're All Insecure, Too

A rtistic expression by its very nature is subjective. If no one recognizes your talent, it hardly matters that you have talent at all. I'm sure there are plenty of amazing artists of every type who toil away in obscurity all over the world. And yet, one of the most expensive pieces of art ever created, Van Gogh's "Sunflowers," looks like something a seventh grader could paint. Actually, most of his art does.

My daughter was doing works like Jackson Pollock's when she was three. But who'd pay a million for her paintings? I still have some if anyone's interested.

So the fact that someone has become successful at what they do artistically is often less tied to pure talent, than to an ability to connect with people in a certain way or at a certain time—what's often referred to as *zeitgeist*—a mysterious capacity or luck in connecting to the cultural movement of a time, which naturally causes an artist's work to be rewarded financially.

It is this unpredictability that causes most artistic people to have a degree of insecurity. It is this reality that will likely cause you to doubt your talent more than anything.

To view it from one angle, the successful people in any business have a special knowledge or ability that the novices lack. It's quite natural, therefore, to believe that a certain talent is missing if success has evaded you. However, in the entertainment business, that's not necessarily the case. Talent levels may be similar, but exposure could be the reason that talent isn't recognized.

The expense of making movies and the elusiveness of knowing what will sell causes studios and prodcos to play things very conservatively in Hollywood. It's comforting to a studio to go with a known actor, writer, or director, for example, as opposed to going with an unknown, in the same way that people often trust a name brand product or think it superior to an unknown brand—even when the ingredients are exactly the same.

The difference between the talent of a star and the unemployed actor or writer may well be little more than opportunity and exposure.

The singing competition *American Idol* exists with the purpose of exposing undiscovered talent to the world. People from all across the country get their chance to be seen. Thousands of highly talented people audition—most of whom you never see.

The ones picked to advance to the next level are not always the best. Two people having similar styles or looks will cause one to be eliminated even though the other is just as good. Only a handful of performers ever get to audition before Randy, Paula, and Simon—the show's hosts. The vast majority audition in huge stadiums with hundreds of other judges.

One judge may like one style while another may not. Or three singers of similar styles in a row makes the third go out the door if the first two have already advanced, even if the third was better—just a matter of timing.

It's like that everywhere in Hollywood. When thousands of scripts, reels or headshots arrive on the desks of readers, agents, and production companies, weeding through them is arduous. The best don't necessarily get noticed. That doesn't mean the talent isn't there. It may just mean more persistence and more diligence are required of the artist in order to get noticed. Keep trying.

Going from being noticed to being a star is a different process for creative artists (writers, composers, painters, choreographers, etc.) and performance artists (singers, actors, dancers, etc.)

It goes without saying that creative artists must create something that is amazing—a mesmerizing book or story, song or musical—something that connects with people emotionally.

Performance artists must find (or make) something amazing and perform it well.

As a writer, I may be prejudiced in my belief about this, but I'm convinced it is the role that creates a movie star, not the other way around. Movie stars get people into seats, but the sheer fact of their being movie stars does not guarantee the movie will be good. It does usually guarantee that people will go see it. And Hollywood executives care about ticket sales far more than story quality. So once someone becomes a star, execs will pay fortunes to have them in their films even if the script is bad. But consider the following...

Al Pacino is a great actor who became a star because of the role of Michael Corleone in *The Godfather*. He'd been in movies before that, but no one remembers him from those. The role of Michael Corleone made him a star.

Sam Jackson has been in movies since 1972—the same year *The Godfather* was made with Pacino. Jackson played all types of characters—some great, some not so great, but he became a star when he got the role of Jules Winnfield in *Pulp Fiction* in 1994—22 years into his career. That role made Sam Jackson a star.

The only stars for which these defining roles are not generally the catalyst to their stardom are comedians. Comedians come to Hollywood to play themselves (or their comedic personas) and they are hired to play themselves in every role. Comedians are both performance and creative artists. First they create a comic persona, and then they perform that persona over and over again in different movies.

Some stars are so defined by their initial star role that they, like comedians, are basically hired to play that same character over and over in different films.

Consider one amazing piece of writing—Quentin Tarantino and Roger Avary's *Pulp Fiction* in 1994. The roles in this film were like a powerful gas nebula cloud that created, recreated and/or altered a host of stars. The stars that this amazing piece of writing created include Sam Jackson, Uma Thurman, and Ving Rhames.

But what's more impressive is that it also recreated the stardom of Bruce Willis, John Travolta, and Christopher Walken.

Bruce Willis, prior to his role in *Pulp Fiction*, could only do goofball comedies and *Die Hard* remakes. After *Pulp Fiction* he was considered a serious dramatic actor and his career went into renaissance.

John Travolta had all but disappeared by the '90s, being so known and pigeonholed for his twenty-something dance phenomenon roles in *Saturday Night Fever* and *Urban Cowboy* (his SNF role basically a cinematic turn on his *Welcome Back, Kotter* TV character, Vinnie Barbarino). But after *Pulp Fiction* his career blossomed such that he could do roles he never knew existed. He still has to dance, but he's so much more now. Post-*Pulp*, his career took off.

Christopher Walken was an amazing dramatic actor who'd even won a Best Supporting Oscar in 1978 for his role as a Vietnam veteran in *The Deer Hunter*. But his role in *Pulp Fiction* was so strong that Walken's deadpan, straight delivery came off as one of the funniest parts of the film. Walken's 42-year career of supporting dramatic performances turned the corner with this role and recreated him as a comedic actor. Moreover, it branded him a star, as he'd never been before.

The great wisdom of Tarantino and Avary that allowed them to transform these stars was their ability to "bridge" the actors' former careers to the new careers they wanted.

Bruce Willis was known for playing crazy, silly, wiseguys. I loved him in *Moonlighting*, and that role was so powerful, it kept him doing that same character even on the big screen in *Die Hard*. For Bruce to work as a serious dramatic actor, he'd have to be a little of his old self mixed in with the new. So, in *Pulp*, he tricks a gangster out of his money, then can't escape because he's obsessed with his dad's watch, which was left on a ceramic kangaroo.

In retrieving that watch, his life turns upside down, before he finally finds redemption. It's old Bruce tied to new Bruce and ... *Voila!* Now he can play a completely serious character in *Sixth Sense*.

Walken's character in *Pulp* was a Vietnam vet—a similar character for which he'd won an Oscar as a dramatic actor. But it was made funny. Now he can do comedy.

Travolta got talked into entering a twist contest—so the audience could see him dance. But he's also reading books, traveling the world and killing people. Now he's a believable gangster and dramatic actor.

The fact of the matter is that it is the role that makes the star, not the other way around. People may say they always like a certain actor's movies, but that's because once the star is born, many more roles come to keep him or her in orbit. Stars get these great roles because they get to see all the scripts first. The stars don't make bad roles great; they get to pick the great roles. But they wouldn't have this ability if they'd not gotten that part that created them in the first place.

Luckily for new actors, the stars can't play every role they get offered. Eventually some great parts will filter down to the ranks of the lesser known. So the goal of any performer looking to become that star is to find that star role.

But the lesson for the creative artist is that stars are always looking for great roles to keep them in orbit. They do have their pick of great scripts, but because everyone is insecure and unsure of what will work theatrically, they may also be open to your script. Getting a script to a star can be a shortcut to your own career. Learning to keep an eye on actors looking to do different roles for which your script may be a bridge could help draw them.

There Are at Least Ten People in Hollywood Who Look, Sing or Act Exactly Like You

I n addition, there are 100 who fit your "type" and can "pull you off" if necessary. Those people will be at every audition you go to.

I once showed up at an audition at Paramount (ironically) and I could tell where I needed to go by the steady stream of men who looked like me. It was surreal. It was as if there was some mad scientist with a mold of me.

When I got in the room, I could hear the others auditioning. They sounded like me. And they sounded like each other. And I wondered what in the world they could be looking for that any of these guys couldn't do.

The part was that of a friend visiting one of the main characters on a sitcom—a single episode, non-recurring role. But it was a speaking part, which meant you became SAG (Screen Actors Guild) eligible because of Taft-Hartley.

Taft-Hartley is a big deal for new actors in this city because it shortcuts you into SAG membership. SAG gets you benefits like health insurance. SAG gets you paid more. And SAG allows you to audition for SAG-only parts—

where the real money is. And, if you're stuck doing "extra" work, it will even get you double the pay for that. Being a member of the guild is the first sign of being a true professional actor.

But the point of this is not how the guild benefits actors, but how Hollywood sees you as a "type."

Hollywood does not see you as an individual. They see you as a type. The only people who are seen as individuals are stars. And some of them are just the biggest types, more so than stars. And it's all about marketing.

If you write, Hollywood insists that you write a certain genre. You must either be a comedy writer, or a dramatic writer, or an adventure writer, or an action writer. You cannot just be a writer who writes whatever he wants.

John Grisham can write nothing but law stories. Stephen King took thirty years to break out of horror. The Beatles would have never produced the variety of song types they did if they had to do it for today's Hollywood—I don't care how much LSD they used.

My first script was dramatic. My second was a comedy. I didn't realize that was taboo. Once I was known as a dramatic writer, no one wanted to read my comedic stuff. Action was okay since action is mostly drama, but comedy seemed to be a bit of a stretch. Whatever you come here doing, be prepared to do it for the rest of your life. Or, if you're a writer, be prepared to write under different names so no one knows it's you.

Actors as well as writers bemoan this situation. Many actors hate not being able to play characters that are outside their genre. And very few actors ever transcend this limitation unless they do it in drag—like Tyler Perry, who pays Madea to big laughs, but plays his male characters seriously.

Other dramatic actors get away with comedy by playing serious in funny situations—this is Walken's secret in *Pulp Fiction* and Jack Nicholson's in *As Good As It Gets*.

But for the most part, if you sing, you must sing in a certain style. It's all about marketing.

Hollywood is about selling product.

You get sold when they know how to sell you. They know how to sell you when you stick to one thing and one thing only.

So just know that if you come here with a comedy script, you're going to have to write another and another and another. If you come here with action, or adventure, or suspense—make sure you love that genre because you will need to keep writing it.

So what's your type? Have you figured it out yet? Do you have a particular genre that you love to write? Do you love comedies, dramas, or action? Pick the one you love the most and write a few scripts in that genre. Don't mix them up figuring you'll shotgun it—nah, that's not the ticket.

Think I'm joking? How's this for narrow? The screenwriter of *The Devil Wears Prada* wrote another screenplay. It also was a comedy. It also had clothing in the title. The name? *27 Dresses*. At least it wasn't *The Devil Wears Gucci, Too!* (Get it? "Too" instead of "2"?). Yeah, it's that bad. Watch and see if something very similar to that doesn't show up in theaters soon.

If you act, have you developed a particular character that you believe you can sell in an audition? Do you come off a certain way that works? Do you have a certain look that you see a lot of on TV? Are you recognizable as a stereotype? Do you look ghetto, or barrio, or Orange County-ish, hillbilly, Mafia, Miami salsa, Russian thuggish, sorta fat white college dropout guy-ish, Arab terrorist, Chinese karate, lesbian, gay, skinny, nerdy, goth, slutty pole dancer-ish, uptight upright conservative fatherly, bookish college student-ish, or Capri pants middle-class housewife-ish? Come on to Hollywood, you'll get an audition every week.

But remember, you have to look the type and act the type. You can't be Mafioso Italian or Colombian looking, and be heady, artsy or smart too. You have to play it dumb and street or you'll just confuse casting directors.

Are you super ugly? Super weird looking? If so, you may have a better chance than the super beautiful—tons of those here. And super beautiful people are out. The everyday Joe look is in.

Are you really tall—over 6'2"? Not good. Average height? Good. Stars can be tall (although most are really short); everyone else, no. You have to fit in, not stand out.

So do yourself a favor before you come here—know your type. Ask friends and family what character you look like or know what you like to write or sing and don't stray from that type—at least not until you're a star.

If You Are Original, There is No Place For You in Hollywood

Along the same lines as the last chapter, you should know that if what you bring is "fresh and new" or "never seen before," it will never be seen here either. No one is going to risk bringing your original vision to screen, stage, or CD.

The newest term I've heard for this type of thinking is the phrase "template for success," as in, "Do we have a template for success to hang this idea on?"

In terms of screenplays, truer words would be, "*Of what successful film or two films*" (if you want to be more original, you combine two films that have already been done) "*is this story a derivative?*"

If you can't answer that question with something like, "It's *Titanic* meets *Rambo*," you're in deep trouble. You can pitch the most original, exhilarating story ever imagined, and if it doesn't boil down to a derivative of two other successful movies, it's most likely going to be kiboshed.

Again, it's all about marketing. Hollywood has to pigeonhole everything so it knows how to sell it. And whether that marketing is the result of people's actual tastes or of marketers' prejudices, this is a sample of what Hollywood believes:

1. A kid who listens to hip-hop would never listen to grunge or rock, and *vice versa*.
2. The people who go to see comedies are not the same people who go to see dramatic movies.
3. Teenagers only want to watch movies about other teenagers.
4. No one in Japan or Europe can stand to look at black people in the movies unless it's Chris Tucker with Jackie Chan.
5. Little girls will go to see a movie starring a boy, but little boys won't go to see a movie starring a girl.
6. No one in America wants to see a black man kiss a black woman—but if he kisses a Latina, sure.
7. Teenagers get more sex than anyone.
8. Married couples never have sex with each other, and all of them are unhappily married and have affairs.
9. White people will not go see black movies unless a few of the key characters are white.
10. No black people ever watched *Seinfeld* or *Frazier* and no white people watched *Martin*.

My point is this. If you have a script in which any of the above rules are violated, be ready for the notes to rewrite it.

If you wrote it that way precisely because your experience is different from what you've been seeing in the movies and you want to bring your experience to the screen, bad move. Go preach in church. Hollywood supports the status quo because it believes it knows how to market it.

I personally came to understand this reality after a meeting at Fox in 2004. I had originally gone to Fox because they were considering me to write the next *Omen*. Prior to the meeting I viewed all the old *Omen* movies—including the one that had impacted me so much as a teenager, *Damien Omen II*. I was actually very excited about the possibility and the coincidence. But when I saw what Fox had done with *Omen 4*, which I had not realized even existed, I told them the franchise was dead in my opinion.[3]

Fox then offered me the opportunity to go through their vault to choose any movie, which Fox had previously made, and then pitch them my take on a prequel, a sequel or a modernization of that film. They explained to me that they were attempting to develop franchise movies like Universal, "...such as *Beethoven*. I mean they can just keep making those things. Which one are they on now, fifteen? We need to do franchises like that."

The point was that such films did not require much in terms of the marketing budget. A studio could place such titles on the shelf of a video store and they would be rented solely based on name recognition. They also didn't require large budgets. Partly because they didn't require stars. The franchise itself was the star.

I didn't like the idea. I came to Hollywood to write original screenplays, not remakes. But I needed the work, so I went online to check out the Fox vault. There were some impressive titles. I went back later for another meeting after I'd chosen *How to Marry a Millionaire*, *The Day The Earth Stood Still*, *The Cannonball Run* and *War of the Roses*. They had excuses for why each wouldn't work.

"Someone's working on *How to Marry a Millionaire*. They've been working on that for years. It's all tied up in legal, I think."

"*Cannonball Run* is too expensive. And War of the Roses is a dark comedy—dark comedies don't do well—especially overseas."

"Spielberg and Cruise are doing *War [of the Worlds]* now--too similar to *Day [the Earth Stood Still]*—probably not a good idea to mess with them."[4]

Everything is about how a movie can be marketed for profit. It is a business far more than a creative endeavor to work in Hollywood.

If you ever wondered why Hollywood makes so many horror movies, it's

---

3 Fox apparently agreed with me because a couple years later, they released **The Omen**, which turned out to simply be a refilming of the original script.

4 Fox will release The Day The Earth Stood Still in December 2008, starring Keanu Reeves. I guess it's far enough away from War of the Worlds now. See WIK 6.

simple. They are cheap and they translate overseas.

Most horror movies are filmed in dark or poorly lit locations—that reduces the cost of sets, decorators, costumes, make up, lighting, locations, and so many other filmic expenses. Horror movies often use very little sound and very few actors compared to many other films. They are the cheapest films. *Saw* takes place in a single room with only a couple actors. Can't get much cheaper than that.

Comedy, apart from slapstick, is often dependent on shared experiences and reference points. These experiences don't often translate to other cultures, but a saw cutting into an arm is universal. It requires no translation and cannot be misinterpreted.

It is for these reasons that action and horror movies are the most universally popular movies. The difference between action and horror though is the cost. Action movies are expensive. They often involve elaborately choreographed fight scenes, chase scenes, crashes, many actors, extras, CGI (computer-generated imagery) and other special effects. All of this takes time. Time for hundreds of professionals equals money. The insurance alone on an action film can cost more than some entire horror movies cost to produce.

Much of the money for making films today comes from overseas banks and financiers. Distributors in overseas markets seek films for their audiences that translate easily and visually. It is the same reason that the most successful foreign films in America are action films and horror films. It is also why the biggest foreign stars in America are foreign action stars.

My point to this WIK is that Hollywood will continue to make what it perceives as the most profitable movies, shows and music. Most profitable does not mean "new," "different," or "unique"—as such is untested and uncertain. What it does mean is "predicable," "clearly marketable" and "widely appealing."

So if you have a feeling that you keep seeing or hearing the same stuff over and over again, it's not just a feeling.

People Here Front Like Mad

I think the term "frontin'" comes from working stock in grocery stores. When an item is running low, stockers are told to move the items to the front of the shelf to make the shelf look full. At first glance, the store appears well stocked and maintained. Upon closer inspection, the truth becomes apparent—there's nothing there. Hollywood is full of people who have nothing there.

You will meet people who will leave you with the impression that they are high rollers—big agents, successful producers, directors, actors, and writers.

But here's a trustworthy rule when it comes to meeting people: If they were all of that, you wouldn't be meeting them. And, if by chance you do meet someone big, you likely won't even know it. The ones who talk are very usually nobodies.

One thing you will notice in L.A. is that you've never seen so many BMWs, Mercedes Benzes, Escalades, and Porsches anywhere outside a dealership in your life.

Everyone drives these things. It's not unusual to see ten Mercedes Benzes turn a corner one right behind another. It's lunacy. It's frontin'. Everyone is dressing for the part. I personally know people who are completely broke but who drive new BMWs in L.A. The mindset here is that you have to look the part. Oddly enough, some of the biggest stars and producers ride around in crappy looking cars with pristine new engines in them so as not to be noticed, but also so as not to break down on the side of the road. It's the laid-back-appear-unaffected-by-it-all look. If you're going for that look, you spend a fortune to look nasty. But if you're not famous, you might want to throw on a $5K+ watch to make sure they know it's just a "look."

But it's not just the cars and the clothes; it's also the scene. One of my first lunch meetings was on the Sunset Strip at Le Petit Four. (In my opinion, the food at these chic industry restaurants is overrated. But then again, people don't really go there for the food.) I was meeting with a couple of producers and their attorney to iron out details of their option of my script.

I can't remember what I ate, but it was ridiculously expensive (even though I wasn't paying for it) and under-flavored. We talked crap for hours—over and over about the same points. I was getting tired, and that's when I realized the producers were trying to be seen.

I noticed because I was too. It felt cool. It was seductive. They were trying not to give me $10K for the option on my script. It had now been over a year we'd been "talking." I couldn't believe it. How could they produce a movie if they couldn't come up with ten grand to option the script? "Was that Charlize Theron?"

Like I said, frontin' is seductive. When I first arrived, I wanted to get a subscription to *Variety*. A subscription cost $480. Ridiculous. But I found out that the producer who was trying to buy my script had a subscription. I asked her for her old copies. She agreed.

I would go by her house on Mondays after my screenwriters' group meeting and get the magazines off her front porch. I kept them on me, at my apartment, in my car—so folk would know I was in the business—Frontin'.

Everyone has a project going on. When they first mention it, it's impressive. Ask a few more questions, though, and you'll find out it's a student film. It's non-paid. It's "in development." It "was" getting made. It's an independent film. It's not the actor/director/producer you're thinking of.

He "used" to be my agent.

Everyone has his or her hustle. "I went to college with him, I don't actually know him now." There's nothing wrong with having a hustle. What's wrong is pretending you're doing more than you are and getting other people to put their energies into your game.

But if people here front, Hollywood itself does it more. Hollywood is the king of over-promising and under-delivering.

Think about how many times you've watched a trailer and then gone to see the movie only to find that the trailer was funnier apart from the film. In context, the "funny" elements were stupid.

How many movies have been billed as "amazing," "laugh-out-loud funny," or "terrifying," only to turn out inept, boring, and ridiculous?

The problem is that it costs millions to make that bad movie so some of that money must be recouped.

It's a good thing therefore that critics often work for the very companies that produce or distribute the movies. Gene Shalit works for *Today*, which is owned by NBC/Universal. I've never seen Gene Shalit—as irascible as he is—*ever* can a Universal pic since Universal merged with NBC. He'll can everything else, but not a Universal movie. Universal movies seem to always be excellent to Gene—even if they suck to everyone else.

And the same goes for all the other media outlets. Fact is, no matter where you're getting your review, or where the quoted review in the trailer originates, it's most likely a reviewer employed by a business that is related to the studio releasing the film and therefore... biased. Amazingly, some films still can't get praise. Those films are unspeakably bad.

So whether someone is frontin' about his or her projects, and/or how connected they are, or Hollywood is frontin' about the quality of a film, it's all evidence of the next thing I WIK...

No One Minds Wasting Your Time

Or maybe it would better be stated that no one gives a crap about your time. However, his or her time is the most precious thing on the planet.

Life in Hollywood is a game of status and power. You're like a new pledge on campus. They don't care that you're missing work, canceling doctor's appointments, missing job interviews, or about to lose your mind in traffic to make it to this meeting. If they want to see your face again—despite having seen it two days ago, having it on video and having two photos of it, they'll make you drive back across the city in rush hour traffic just to look at you and say, "Nah, go with the other guy." Even if the other guy could be your twin brother.

Casting directors have no problem booking 100 people for the exact same audition time. They have no problem locating their offices in buildings that have no parking anywhere near them. They don't care that you're traveling twenty or thirty miles to say two lines. They don't care that there are only two lines and they already know they're going to cast their cousin in the part and not you. They just don't care.

I thought of sharing the story about my meeting with the producer I mentioned in the intro of this book for a later time, but it fits well here.

This particular producer had scheduled and cancelled a pitch meeting on me two times in a row. Well, the third one's the charm, they say. So this story starts at the point where we're finally going to meet. I'm pasting it directly from the e-mail I sent to my writing group:

> *I walk into the office and tell the receptionist (a young English woman) that I'm there for Larry and Gil. She says "Larry's not back yet, but I'll let Gil know", Then asks if I'd like some water, juice, whatever. I say water.*
>
> *"So, you're a writer?"*
>
> *"Yes."*
>
> *"Wow, cool. You here to... what? Pitch a story?"*
>
> *"Yeah."*
>
> *"What's it about?"*
>
> *"I figure it's a great time to practice, so I pitch it. "It's Finding Forrester meets National Treasure, blah, blah, blah..."*
>
> *"Really? I just can't imagine why someone would want to make a movie like that. It couldn't possibly do any business overseas. I mean, the whole black/white thing is such an American phenomenon, isn't it? We certainly don't have issues like that in England."*
>
> *I'm stunned, but I recover well. First, because they sure as hell do have issues like that in England and secondly because she's a receptionist, right?*
>
> *"With regards to race, maybe. But everyone has someone living in the neighborhood who's different from everyone else... kinda mysterious. And it's an adventure movie."*
>
> *"I suppose. But what I'm passionate about is women. Does it have many women in it? You know, white women between the ages of 40 and 55 are the most under-represented demographic in films. The most over-represented is young black men."*

I obviously don't live on the same planet as this woman. Her planet sounds interesting though.

"I'd go see anything with Julia Roberts in it," she said.

"Did you see Runaway Bride?"

"Oh, I didn't li... Why? Did you write it?"

"No."

"Well it wasn't her best work."

"Funny that women would be a majority of the audience and yet there's only one or two who have proven they can open a film—mainly Sandra Bullock. Even Julia and Meg Ryan seem to need other stars," I reminded her.

"Well, there's nothing catty about that."

Enter a tall white...man, "T.R., I'm Jason, Larry's assistant." He stops a few feet away with his hand extended, hanging loosely from his wrist, seeming to beckon me to follow him. I stand, move towards him and shake his hand. "Larry's finishing up on the phone now, and when he does, you can come on back. So just hang here a sec."

I sit back down thinking how weird it was that he didn't just come the other 3 feet to shake my hand instead of making me get up.

Bridget Jones pipes up again. I notice there is a stack of scripts in front of her and I realize she also reads for the production company. I'm thinking God help whoever wrote those. They'd better have a role for Julia.

"More films like Ya Ya Sisterhood need to be made," she insisted.

I ask if it did well at the box office. She says she doesn't think so. I tune her out and try to figure out how Larry got into the office without me seeing him.

Before I get that figured out Gil comes out. "Hey T.R., good to see you again. Larry couldn't make it in. He hurt his foot this morning, but he wanted to keep the appointment this time. Sorry about the cancellations. He's going to meet over the phone."

I pitch badly in person. I'm insufferable on the phone. And I'm starting to realize I'm pissed off. I drove all the way across town to talk on the phone? You didn't know he hurt his foot earlier? You couldn't call me and have me pitch on the phone from home?

We get to Gil's office. Gil dials Larry up. Larry answers. "Hi, T.R.. Sorry I couldn't be there." I try to adjust. I tell him my manager says hi and try some small talk—warm up to the guy. He says to tell Peter hi and then... "So whatcha got?"

There was no ice broken at all. Not only is this asshole chillin on his Barcalounger somewhere, but he's ruckin' fushing me. So I start into it. "It's basically a story about the mysterious last white man living in a black neighborhood and that white man is Jack Nicholson."

"Ah... I wonder why they thought of us for this?" he says sarcastically. Gil smiles. No doubt because he's the one who thought Larry would love to do it. But it took me a minute to figure out what he said because it was a cheap speaker phone with a voice activated mike and the first couple words get cut off as the mike switches back and forth. "Yeah, okay, go on."

"Well...," I started.

"... the minimum age this guy has to be?"

"What?"

"... got to be how old? What's the minimum? You don't mind me cutting you off like this do you?"

"No"

"... there?... T.R."

"I'm having trouble with the voice activation. I'm missing the first part of everything you're saying."

"... voice... yeah, the phone. Yeah, there's that pause."

"Yeah."

"...ah. So what's the minimum age?"

And it only gets worse from there. It ends with they'd love to see the script when it's written, but it doesn't sound like something they'd want to develop. He loved my sample script. Blah blah blah, tell Peter hi. If you've got anything else to pitch, you and Gil can go over it after I hang up. Again, sorry I couldn't be there. "Nice to meet you."

After Larry disconnects, Gil says, "Hmm. I thought you were going to have it all beat out scene by scene?"

"I do. But it sure didn't sound like that's what he wanted to hear. I was thrown off by the phone and everything."

"Yeah, sorry about that. He hurt his foot this morning..." Like I didn't hear that the first two times. I figured I'd chalk it up to experience. I called my agent on the way home.

He apologized and said, "You may have a bad pitch, but it doesn't mean you're a bad writer. There'll be other pitches," which was encouraging. I called my manager and he said it was a shame. I told him I doubted they intended to do anything from the jump because he'd canceled the meeting twice previously. I figured Gil was just trying to be nice and didn't want to do the dirty work of saying no.

He agreed. Then he said, "And what's worse, Larry was probably sitting in another room in the office the whole time."

Am I serious, you ask? Yes. Imagine driving forty-five minutes across town only to talk on the phone with someone after they've already cancelled on you twice. Amazing arrogance.

I had a meeting with John Woo's company earlier that week. John Woo, as in *Mission Impossible II* John Woo. They never cancelled. They were on time. They met me in person. They didn't criticize my ideas. In fact, they asked to see everything I wrote. So not everyone is bad. Had a meeting with John Wells' company the next week—very courteous.

John Woo's office is twenty miles away in Santa Monica. John Wells' is on the Warner Bros. lot in Burbank.

Both meetings were in order to "meet-n-greet." This is where a producer or one of the producer's underlings sets a meeting with a writer whose work they've read and liked. The purpose of these meetings, as far as I can tell, is to pull you away from whatever important thing you had planned that day and waste a few hours of your time.

Meet-n-greets are supposed to be beneficial to the new writer. But as far as I can tell, they are no different than calling a plumber to your house to see if you like how he smells just because you heard he smelled good at your friend's house.

People in Hollywood fancy themselves to be that important. They say they want to know if they can work with you or not, so they set these meetings to "check you out."

In reality, they want free ideas. They want your pitches. They want you to tell them what you think about their movie ideas. They loved your script, but they don't want to make it. They know you're smart though and that you can write, so why not pick your brain for an hour or so?

I have left more of these meeting scratching my head and wondering, "what the hell was that about?" They didn't need to make me drive across town to tell me they want to read anything else I write. Hell, I already know that. More importantly, my agent already knows that—you're currently on his list of people he sends scripts to, right? Why would he take you off? When I write my next script, you'll get one. You don't have to meet me to tell me you want to see it.

That's exactly why that's not the reason they meet you. I believe they meet you to steal ideas.

Ever wonder why, whenever a big movie comes out, there are three movies just like it from three different studios? I first noticed it back in 1997 with *Dante's Peak* and *Volcano*. Then there was *Armageddon* and *Deep Impact* and another TV movie called *Asteroid* or something.

They say these "same movie-different name" situations are "accidental" or just the result of the *zeitgeist*. That's a lie. They are the results of ideas that have been pitched, and stolen. I'll guarantee you after the writer pitched those ideas he was told, "We're not interested because we already have something similar to that in production." Yeah. They do now.

Screenwriting books argue that studios don't make money stealing ideas because of the threat of being sued. Really? Good luck with suing a studio over a pitch.

Like I said before, these producers are some of the brightest people on the planet. And they are gamblers. Pitching these guys your best ideas is giving them your best ideas. They will turn and pitch it to someone else and forget all about you, then hire a writer to write it and control it better when it's their own, rather than worry about your vision. On top of that, these guys can move from one prodco to another and pitch your idea to anyone and sell it. You'll never trace it back to the source.

The only ideas they won't steal are ones no one else could write. If your uncle worked for the CIA and told you a bunch of stuff no one else knows, and they want to make that film, you'll get the writing job. Otherwise, if they steal your idea, they'll change a bit here and there—it will take place in L.A. instead of New York, the villain will drive a '79 Regal instead of a '78 Impala etc.—but you will recognize it.

Whether you are a writer or actor or anyone trying to break into this business, beware that a lot of time can be spent running to and fro with high hopes, only to find you're wasting your time.

You may be asking, what happens in a "meet-n-greet?" Well, since you'll likely attend them anyway, here's what you can expect:

You will show up at an impressive office. I've never seen a producer who didn't dwell in swanky digs—except the ones who work for studios. If the office is cheaply furnished, it's because it's a block from the beach and they're trying to give that laid-back-appear-unaffected-by-it-all vibe. Usually though, there will be couches, posters of movies they've made—no matter how good or bad—and displays of any awards.

The receptionist will offer you water. An assistant will meet you first. You will be ushered into the inner sanctum and the producer will either be on the phone, hanging up from a phone call, or not yet in the room. You will wait. You will look around and recognize a few films. Pics of stars with the producer may line the walls.

If you meet with the producer alone, they don't mean business. It's a pure butt-sniffing meeting and you are wasting your time. If you meet with the producer and the Creative Director, or the Development Director, they are seriously considering you for something they have in mind, or you are smoking hot. Relax. They will break the ice when they are ready.

The biggest person in the room (the producer) will introduce the smaller folks, if any, and then tell you they loved "[insert the name of your script]." He will talk about how easy it was to read, how well the characters were developed. He will talk about how gripping it was—he couldn't put it down. He will ask you what your inspiration was and what your background is. He will reassure you that you are going to blow up. But he will not buy your script. Don't expect it or ask.

Depending on how talkative you are you may find he's from the same part of the country as you. Or you may find you know someone in common. It doesn't matter. That's not why you're there. Eventually, he will tell you what he's working on currently. And he may ask about other projects you're working on. Be very careful.

What you will notice is that he will describe next to nothing about what he's doing. The only thing you may learn is the title. This is the most revealing part of why you're there. If he was truly excited about what he was working on, why wouldn't he tell you?

You might get a title if it's already famous—"We're doing *Doom*." "We're doing *Like Mike 2*." "We're looking through the vault to see what we might do with a new twist." "We're working on this new reality show like *The Bachelor*, except he's running for President." Most likely it will be even more vague, "We're finishing up a project with [insert a star's name here]." Or, "We're developing some new stuff."

Regardless of what he says, it's what he asks next that is the most dangerous part: "So what other ideas or stories do you have?" He is fishing. He is fishing to steal your ideas. Do not doubt it. You may choose to give them to him—hoping he may hire you to develop them. He won't. Or you can be just as vague as he was. It's up to you.

You will share them because you don't believe me, and you think you're "the one." If it's a good idea, he will plunge deep into the story with you. He will ask questions, laugh, ask more questions, and laugh more. He will ask about character, plot twists, and how it ends. And finally, he will ask how far along you are. If you tell him it's finished, he should ask to read it.

If you tell him you have an outline, he may tell you he wants to see it when you're done. If you say it's just a pitch, he may steal it whole.

More likely, he will steal a scene, a plot or subplot idea, or some intriguing unique aspect of your story or one of your characters to help improve a film he's already working on.

Whether they do this on purpose or your ideas just sink into their subconscious and accidentally pop out as their own brilliant ideas in later meetings, just know you will start seeing the ideas you pitched in films at the Cineplex.

Regardless of what happens, you will not walk out of this meeting with a deal to write a script, nor with a check for a script. You will only walk out with a story to tell and a name to drop to your friends, who will be very impressed if they've never had one of these meetings.

I've never had a meet-n-greet as an actor. I don't think producers do this for actors. I did have something like this with a casting agent once. It was much shorter. He just looked at me, took a pic and said he wanted to use me for something one day soon. He did. He called me back more than ten times for commercials and TV roles and booked me on two commercials.

For the most part, actors do the meet-n-greets at parties. But I suppose meet-n-greets do lead to the next thing I WIK...

Everyone Knows Someone Big In The Business. So What?

When I first arrived in Hollywood, I was so excited to locate my first screenwriting class. What was most exciting is that an actual screenwriter taught it. Let's call him Mort (not his real name).

Mort's flyer said that his class provided "support, mentoring, education, agent and manager introductions and industry contacts." Wow. It went on to say he was a successful Hollywood screenwriter and listed among his credits the original *Island of Dr. Moreau* and *Goin' South*, which starred Jack Nicholson. I quickly forked over my $100 and excitedly began my "mentorship."

The group met (and still continues to meet) in the living room of the screenwriter's West Hollywood "million dollar home." It's impressive. The fact that he bought it thirty years ago (at the same time his movies were made) for $48K was lost on us. The fact it hadn't been changed a bit in those thirty years was lost on us too. It was worth over a million now and it made him look successful.

But not only was he successful, he was "best friends with Jack Nicholson" and he never let you forget it either.

"Me and Jack." "Jack and I." "Over at Jack's house." "Jack's not like that." "Oh, we're very close." "I was with Jack then."

There was a photo—a recent one—of Jack and Mort featured prominently in a display on the piano in his living room. (I've often wondered if Jack displayed the same photo in his living room.)

Next to that photo was a headshot of Mort's "star student" Shane Black. Shane made history selling a script for *The Long Kiss Goodnight* for $4M during the spec script boom. He broke through writing *Lethal Weapon* in '87—and survived off writing all the *Lethal Weapons* since (remember, only action movies if that's what you start with). Shane played Hawkins in *Predator* and he played the café manager in *As Good As It Gets*.

Whether or not Shane was ever one of this guy's students or not, is still a mystery. Every month or so he promised he was going to "bring Shane in to talk to you guys," but he never did. Jack never came either.

Mort met Jack before Jack was Jack—before *Chinatown* and *One Flew Over The Cuckoo's Nest*, the roles that made Jack a star—back almost twenty years earlier when Mort was an actor and Jack and he appeared in *Little Shop of Horrors* together. They became fast friends. Jack's career blew up. Mort is glad he held on because he's made his living off of knowing Jack Nicholson ever since.

Don't get me wrong; Mort's a nice guy. He's an interesting and often dramatic teacher—an actor at heart. His home has a nice artsy vibe. But I didn't learn how to improve my writing there. Instead, the group met and talked. We reviewed each other's scripts despite most of us knowing little about writing—let alone critiquing writing. After members of the class finished guessing at why a terrible script was so bad, Mort would pause dramatically before heaping great bales of praise on the script, leaving the poor student, and the rest of us, hopelessly confused.

Every so often he would interject a Jack story or talk about having studied under the great Lajos Egri—that was Mort at his best.

But don't think that he'll ever introduce you to Jack, or that you'll ever meet any agents or managers, or that you'll do anything other than feed him $100/mo. for as long as you attend the meeting.

Let me take that back. He did have two big meetings where folk showed up. One was a TV writer, who'd actually taken his class at one time, who'd gotten herself on the last season of the *Cosby Show* and then went on to create another show. The other was the producer of *Sex and the City*, who happened to live next door and was doing the meeting as a favor. So he did keep his word about industry contacts. Neither of the visitors took scripts from students, though.

It's kind of like that out here—people know people. It's not really something to be impressed by.

The producer who originally wanted to make my script when I was still in Chicago made it a point to tell me that her producing partner's husband worked with Ice Cube and Dr. Dre as a music producer. She also made a point of telling me that one of her best friends was this woman who had a part in a movie that was in theaters at the time. When I was in Chicago, knowing someone who knew any kind of TV or film actor or whatever was a big deal.

I think that's how it is for most people new to the business. You meet someone who tells you they know this actor from a TV show or a movie, and you freak out. You just assume that you've hit the motherlode and the doors are going to start opening like crazy. You assume this person is close to the business and can really help you. Watch out. More often than not, the name-dropping is to try to control you or your material and the name-droppers are no closer than you are to the person whose name they dropped.

Fact is, if you move to L.A. and do anything or go anywhere, you're bound to run into a star or two.

To make ends meet, a couple years after my wife and I arrived here, we got into real estate—she in sales, me in mortgages. The first listing she got was for a condo owned by one of the members of Boyz II Men. The mother of one of our daughter's friends referred the singer's wife.

On the morning of the first open house, my wife had me go by their condo to help finance any potential buyers. To my surprise, the owners stayed for the open house. I was excited. I wasn't a big Boyz II Men fan, but they were all right with me. There I was sitting in the living room talking with one of the biggest selling pop singers in history—just chatting it up about what they were doing now and a movie he'd produced, that was actually pretty decent and a favorite of my daughter's.

In the hallway downstairs were his Grammys and AMAs (American Music Awards, for those who don't know) and an Image Award from the NAACP—very impressive. He was a nice guy. While we were talking, a Boyz II Men song came on the radio station we were listening to. That was a trip. I hadn't noticed until he started singing along and I actually thought, "Wow, he sounds just like the song." Duh.

Oddly, he lived in an 1800 square foot condo—only 700 square feet bigger than our apartment. I figured, if this guy is living here, how much money do the people who live in the big houses have?

But what was wild was that the first person to show up at the open house that morning was Cindy Williams of *Laverne and Shirley*. Now Boyz II Men is famous to me. But Cindy Williams was famous to both of us from our childhood. So here I am watching this famous musician, himself, star-struck over this television icon. It was surreal, to say the least. I mean, this woman knew The Fonz.

I give her the tour of the condo. He follows behind us. I'm freaking out. He's freaking out. We're both goo-gooing over how we loved her show and trying to remember, "What was that lyric they used to sing at the beginning?"

"Hasenpfeffer Incorporated."

"Really? I'd always thought it said 'House of Shotz Incorporated' because they worked for Shotz Brewery."

She's asked if the LCD TVs in the kitchen stay with the condo. "Whatever you want, Shirley—I mean Cindy."

She didn't buy the condo because the noise from the street was too loud, even with the window closed. My wife sold it instead to a woman who worked at a porn magazine—I'd forgotten L.A. was the center of that industry too.

After we sold their place, they invited us to their twin babies' birthday party. Because they hadn't found their new place yet, the party was held at a park inside the gated community of Beverly Park, as the guests of Martin Lawrence—the singer's wife worked for Martin.

Talk about an experience. Paparazzi flew in helicopters overhead to try to take pics of the event. Eddie Murphy's daughter was there. So were Martin Lawrence and his family. Denzel Washington and Sam Jackson are neighbors, along with Eddie, who lives right across the street from Martin in this ridiculously large house. Rod Stewart lives next door. Magic Johnson lives up the way. Avi Arad, Sly Stallone, Tim McGraw, Faith Hill and Barry Bonds all have homes there as do Reba McEntire and Sumner Redstone. I could probably make a decent living off the paper route in that neighborhood.

It was the two-year-olds' birthday party but all the gift bags were from Tiffany and Chanel. Our mouths spent a good deal of time wide open in awe.

My point is, in L.A. it's not hard to meet celebrities, take pics with them, and pretend you know them better than you do. If they're black, you can probably meet them in somebody's church on Sunday—Stevie Wonder and some of the women from Destiny's Child are just as likely to be singing as anyone else. If they're white, you can catch them on the beach in Malibu or shopping in West Hollywood.

For dinner at Mr. Chow's in celebration of my birthday, my wife and daughter and I sat between the overly tanned host of *Entertainment Tonight* and Katie Holmes. The paparazzi waited in ambush outside.

Celebrities live here and they pop up everywhere. They pretend they don't like the attention, but of course that's not true. If they didn't like the attention, they wouldn't come around us normal people.

My point in this WIK is that lots of folk in Hollywood know people who are huge in the industry, but you shouldn't kid yourself about them being able to or willing to help you. The fact that anyone you know actually knows them means nothing to you or the advancement of your career, so don't waste your time or embarrass yourself by kissing their asses.

I believe I can honestly say that I know people who know anyone and everyone you'd ever want to know, but they will never risk those relationships to do a favor for you unless there's something very significant in it for them. Why? Because ...

Everyone Is Watching Their Own Butt

Your butt matters only to the extent that it can immediately save or help theirs. That person with the famous friend will not get your script or your headshot to their famous producer, actor, writer, or director friend unless they know doing so will help them move up or stay up. If there is a chance at all that that famous friend will react negatively towards your material, it won't get passed on. And those friends of the rich and powerful will sometimes waste months of your time getting you to revise material to the point they feel it's worthy to pass on, but it will never be so worthy.

One thing can be said about folk in Hollywood—they all know that other folk out here are fickle and that the business is very volatile. This is the primary reason producers and executives won't take chances on unproven talent. It's also the reason the star system is so completely outrageous.

Movies today cost $100M to make and market. Even a lower budget film runs $5-10M and cost two times that to market. If an executive loses that kind of money, he or she can easily land on the chopping block. The best defense they have against losing that money is hiring known talent—proven moneymakers.

That explains why so many films now go into the $100M range to produce—they have to pay the star talent. And having star talent is the only way to make sure the blame doesn't fall back onto the executive. It's the best way to insure that people will buy tickets.

So a movie needs to star Tom Hanks, Tom Cruise, Denzel Washington, Johnny Depp, Angelina Jolie, or Halle Berry, or be directed by Spielberg, Lucas (only if it's *Star Wars*), Bay, Woo, or be written by the writers who wrote this hit or that hit (screenwriters are rarely famous outside Hollywood, except book authors and playwrights. For instance, had you ever heard of David Koepp or known what he'd written? David Mamet, sure, but because of his plays, not his screenwriting. In Hollywood movie ads, they are known as "the writers of..."), or the movie has to be based on this famous book, a famous video game, a big news event, etc.

It's so ridiculous it's getting to the point where I'm sick of seeing the same actors all the time. As I write this, Denzel just came out playing Frank Lucas—a gangster—in *American Gangster* and a college professor in *The Great Debaters*, both within a couple months.

I notice Will Smith completely vanishes every year until his films come out, and then he's everywhere. *I Am Legend* hit theaters and during the previews ads for his 2008 summer movie, *Hancock,* ran.

It's kind of weird seeing the billboard for the next movie an actor is in while he's still in the one playing in the theater. IMDB says Will has two more slated. Go, Will, go. Considering he gets $20M a flick plus 20% of gross, studio execs are definitely willing to pay to protect their asses.

Brad Pitt has three films for 2008, three for 2009 and, so far, two for 2010. Of course, the year isn't over yet: that 2010 spot will no doubt fill up soon.

But to top them all, Martin Lawrence just came out with *Welcome Home, Roscoe Jenkins,* and the following week came out with *College Road Trip*—two movies in the theaters at the same time? Now that's star power.

Actors do this because they have no idea how long their careers will last. They could completely fall out of favor tomorrow and find themselves having to do *Celebrity Survivor* to make ends meet or to be able to afford to stay in their 20,000 square foot mansions.

A drug habit can wipe out a fortune. So can a bad accountant. So can a lawsuit. They know this business is fickle, so they watch their own butts. The same is true for everyone else. And that brings me to another "Wish I Knew"...

The Industry of "Getting You Into The Industry" Is Almost as Big as the Industry Itself

H ere's a tidbit to keep in mind as you wander through the tables at the National Screenwriters Convention—people lead seminars, teach classes, run courses, do boot camps and workshops, and so on, because they make good money doing so. They're not so driven to see you succeed, but they are driven to have a gig to keep them afloat until *they* succeed.

The person who's running the seminar is usually nothing more than the actor, writer, director, or producer who's been in Hollywood a couple years longer than you have and hasn't made it yet, but has learned a few things more than you currently know.

Ask them what they've sold. If they haven't sold anything, ask them why they feel qualified to teach a class. If they have sold, make sure it's been in the last decade or so. And make sure it's been produced. Selling a script to your uncle for $10 just to say you sold one shouldn't qualify you to run a seminar.

One of the things you'll notice soon after arriving is the incredible amount of these support networks and workshops that exist to help you hone your craft and "break into" the industry. Some of these places have been around for as long as Hollywood has been around.

At best, these classes can put you in touch with like-minded artists that can really help you develop your skills. At worst, they will take your money and feed you fluff. If you attend and get the sinking feeling that they are teaching you something very formulaic and unbending or that they don't seem to really know what they're talking about, or they're impatient, or they have a drug problem—get out.

This is true not only in Hollywood, but around the country. Every town has some place that offers seminars or training in the arts.

I mentioned my screenwriting class at Columbia College in Chicago earlier. My "professor" for that class vanished halfway into the semester—this was after he swore he loved my stuff, so I was curious as to what happened to him. It turned out he was a drug addict. My wife and I saw him on the street weeks later and offered him a ride home. We learned that the reason he'd disappeared was because he was held hostage in someone's basement.

I love crazy people, so we exchanged numbers. He often popped by my office to chat or ask for money. That's when I found out he was an addict. After I lost my money in the stock market, he referred me to his therapist, who helped me embrace the Buddhist concept of "having and not holding," which went a long way towards helping me get past my loss—and still does when things don't go well today.

I mention him only because I later found out that he was fired from Columbia because he'd lied about his credentials. He didn't have a Master's from Boston College, nor had he optioned any scripts to Hollywood.

He did, however, make a huge show of departing the "decrepit city of Chicago" (as he called it) for a writing gig in L.A., only to return two months later with the story that the male producer who'd invited him there only wanted him for sex. Apparently, his credentials weren't the only questionable ones.

Back to Hollywood...

At some point you and/or your spouse and/or your child will be stopped by someone in the grocery store, shopping mall, school or gas station, and asked if you act or model. You'll feel flattered. Don't be. Everyone gets asked that. If you say yes, you'll then be asked if you have an agent. If you say no, they will suggest that you try it and give you the number of a place to call or visit. Don't go unless you want to waste a few days of your time and spend hundreds of dollars on headshots—unless you find that kind of thing cool and interesting. Just tell them you already have an agent and they'll leave you alone.

Headshots are a big business in Hollywood. Everyone has a headshot because everyone has run into the people referenced above. The photographs cost a fortune and don't mean anything, because every casting agent has an assistant who will Polaroid you at the audition and staple that retarded fisheye Polaroid close-up to your glamorous headshot.

If you have to have a headshot, only get it from photographers who have headshots signed "Thank you" by actors you actually recognize. However, you'd do well to verify that actor's signature first.

Also, make sure you do not print the name of your agent on your headshots. Agents prefer that you do this for the sole purpose of making it expensive for you to leave them. Printing their name and info on the front of your headshots means those headshots are only good for use with that agency. If you change agencies, you'll have to pay for new prints. You should print their info instead on the attached resume because you don't want leaving them to be expensive, and you don't want them to think it will be either.

So, unless your agency pays for your headshots—and they won't—don't let them tell you to put their name on them because...

Percenters (Agents, Managers and Lawyers) Are Overrated

When I first came to Hollywood, I was convinced that all I needed to do was get a good agent and the world would be mine. That's because it seemed no one would read anything unless it came from an agent. No one would see you unless you had an agent. No one took you seriously unless you had an agent.

But the catch-22 was that no agent would read your stuff unless someone they knew referred you to them, or if you already had an agent and were trying to change agents, or if you'd already been hired to write or work and the agent was just coming in to make his ten percent. I was obsessed with getting an agent.

Fortunately for me, I had a relationship with a fairly well-known entertainment attorney. Let me mention here that entertainment attorneys in Hollywood are not hired the same way as attorneys in other fields. An entertainment attorney is a type of representative (more like an agent) who is paid a percentage (usually 5% of whatever he's negotiating on your behalf). Thus a $10,000,000 contract nets an entertainment attorney half a million in fees. These aren't the kind of guys who place Yellow Pages ads. At least not the ones with the kind of contacts you would need to get an agent.

So how'd I get that relationship? Saw his name in a book, called his office and got a fax number and faxed him a letter explaining that I was new to the business, had just been a semi-finalist in the Chesterfield, had a producer trying to buy my script and I was looking for a good attorney. He said he repped new talent, but that I needed an agent too and immediately gave me the names of three agents. To my utter surprise, one was Larry David's agent, Richard Arlook. Larry, of course, is the creator of *Seinfeld* and *Curb Your Enthusiasm*. I was blown away. Another was Alan Gasmer of William Morris, whom I'd read about in a book on spec scripts—he'd negotiated one of the biggest spec script sales in history.

A spec script is a full script written on speculation—without pay—and submitted for sale with the hope that someone will buy it.

In the early '90s, there was a boom in spec scripts, due to what some believed was the ridiculous expense of developing scripts in-house. Studios bought spec scripts for millions and it was all over the papers that a number of Hollywood screenwriters were making crazy money on spec scripts. I have to admit, it's part of what fueled my desire to write screenplays. A spec script is also the way that a new writer gets an agent or a writing job with a prodco.

All three agents graciously read my script. All three also graciously turned me down. I faxed another letter to the attorney mentioning my rejection and got three more agent's names.

I got a meeting with one—we had complimentary apples together in the lobby of the Four Seasons Beverly Hills. It was my first big Hollywood meeting.

I was in town on vacation and considering moving here. The agent suggested we "get something to eat" at the Four Seasons. I'd never been to the Four Seasons, though I'd heard Oprah praise it for giving its guests full-sized bars of soap. High class. So it was a huge deal for me. I had no idea what to expect, how to dress, how to behave. I was excited and nervous all day long as I prepared to meet him. I felt lucky. Here I was coming to Hollywood for the first time and already I had a dinner meeting with an agent from a major agency. This was all so cool, so dream-like, and so perfect. Or so I thought.

He came in, walked right to me as if he'd met me before, introduced himself, shook my hand and ushered me past the dining room entrance to a side lobby with a white couch and chair. We sat and he ate an apple that he had plucked from a bowl on the table. He offered one to me as if he'd brought them with him—or perhaps he thought I didn't know they were complimentary? Or perhaps he wanted me to believe he'd reserved that part of the lobby for our meeting and had ordered the apples especially for this occasion? Or maybe he just didn't like eating apples alone or was just being nice. Either way, I felt no desire or obligation to indulge in their red deliciousness. Besides, this couldn't possibly be what he meant by "get something to eat" and I didn't want to ruin my appetite.

For fifteen minutes he bemoaned the fact that he didn't much like being an agent. He told me he had formerly been VP of Business Affairs for Universal. I just looked him up—he's now a VP at Mattel. At the time we met, though, he was an agent with Broder-Kurland.

I thought he was impressed with my writing and that was why he wanted to meet me. Over the course of the conversation it dawned on me that not only were we not going to join the other guests in the dining room as I'd anticipated, but that he'd not yet read my script. He simply didn't want to miss me just in case I was a great writer—since I was only going to be in town a few days.

Amazing. I'd fought two hours of traffic on the 405 freeway to meet him there at 5:30 p.m. – the height of rush hour. He strolled in, ate and apple, checked his Patek Philippe watch and strolled back out before 6pm.

Since then, I've come to refer to all such pointless meetings—be they with agents, producers, or prodcos as "having apples at the Four Seasons."

When I returned to Chicago, he had my script read, sent me the coverage, and turned me down. So did the other agents. I was discouraged. My lawyer contact fed me a few more agents, then said I could send it to any agency saying he referred me. I did.

Everyone read it. CAA gave me great coverage and a "recommend," but chose not to take me on. William Morris gave my script a recommend too, despite the fact that Gasmer had turned it down previously.

"Coverage" is what happens to scripts when they get submitted anywhere in Hollywood.

Basically, a reader is paid to read the script and determine if it's a good story either for the company, the agency, or the producer—i.e., whether it's what they're looking for to produce, or to set up with an actor they have under contract. The reader also judges whether you're a good writer. In essence, the coverage saves the agents, producers and executives time.

Readers break down into two types: "Wannabe Producer Readers" and "Wannabe Screenwriter Readers."

Wannabe producer readers are usually employed by production companies and are fixed on their preset ideas of the kinds of movies they want to see made or that their companies want to make. Whether they like your script or not is completely based on whether your script meets those criteria or not. For example, the receptionist/reader I mentioned earlier, "Is it a good star role for Julia Roberts? I want to work with her." Poor Julia. Or in the case of your script falling into that reader's hands and not having a role for Julia, poor you—their coverage on your script will be negative.

If, however, your script has an interesting role for Julia, and it falls into that reader's hands, you may find yourself being courted even if your script needs work.

Producers look for ideas for stories. Producers look for roles for actors with whom they have or want a relationship. Producers look for movies that are cheap to produce or can be produced within a certain budget. Producers look for something specific and if your script happens to be that thing, you are golden. (By the way, the main role of an agent is to know what producers are looking for and to find it first or know where to get it. Agents get paid by making those connections.)

Sadly though, a true disservice is done when a reader cans a script just because it's not what the company is looking to produce. Writers dread coverage, and bad coverage could stop a good new writer and a good story from being submitted elsewhere. Seasoned writers know these realities and shrug off rejection more easily, but new writers are vulnerable to second-guessing style, skill and their callings as writers. Many good writers have packed up their bags and left Hollywood or stopped presenting their writing to the world because of unwarranted negative criticism.

Why do you think so many studios rejected *Star Wars* and *E.T.*? The writing wasn't horrible. Those stories simply weren't what the studios or productions companies were looking to do. But I'd love to read the coverage—I'll bet that the readers bashed those scripts unfairly.

Wannabe screenwriter readers are a different breed. I know some of them personally from various screenwriting groups. These are people who want the very job I want—they are my competition. They are often employed by agencies to do general reviews of screenplays. They take those jobs in hopes of sneaking in a few of their own scripts when the time is right.

Now imagine a highly competitive and subjectively judged sport, such as gymnastics. Let's pretend I compete in gymnastics and I also get to judge those who will be competing against me. The ones I judge, however, have no knowledge of my participation in the competition or my skill level and furthermore, they will not sit in judgment of me. In fact, they assume that because I am a judge, I am a non-participant and therefore non-biased. You get the risk here? Good. Do you think it would be fair to compete in gymnastics against me under such circumstances?

If so, you have more faith in me than I do. But consider that I may have often been unfairly judged myself and maybe I don't feel so bad about ripping you apart. Either way, it will likely take a pretty impressive performance to earn my respect.

In terms of competition among writers in Hollywood, very few new writers get in simply because there are so many established ones still looking for work every week. Writing, unlike a regular job, is temporary by its nature. You write for one show until it goes off the air. Or you're hired to write, polish or punch up a script and when you're done, you're unemployed again.

Hollywood writers are constantly looking for work. Only the best ones have projects lined up waiting for them. If you interview for a writer spot on a TV show, you may find yourself competing against scribes who wrote for *Hawaii Five-O* in the '70s, *Cheers* in the '80s, or *X-Files* in the '90s. Many of those folks are still around and still writing. Is it any wonder that it is hard to get into this field? A writer may show age, but not the same way that an actor does. And some writing styles are classic and never go out of favor.

Finally, readers get only about $50 to read a script. That's not much. Many readers read 2-3 a day or more to try to make ends meet or simply because of the sheer number of scripts they must evaluate for their company. When you read that many stories a day, characters, plots and themes can run together in your mind. On top of that, some readers are just lazy or indifferent. Some are jaded. Some get off by rejecting other writers. And a few may have pawned off the job to their nephew for $10 and then wrote coverage based on junior's synopsis.

Whatever may happen in the process, at the end of the coverage, the reader makes a suggestion to "pass", "consider", or "recommend." And remember, if these guys recommend a script and the agent hates it, then they risk not being hired to read any more, and the chances of sneaking in one of their scripts goes out the window. It's much, much easier and safer to suggest a "pass" than a "consider" or "recommend," and it cuts down on the competition to boot. Consider this quote from *Inside Film Magazine*:

> 'RECOMMEND,' which was never freely given, has become nearly extinct on script coverage. Even if a reader really likes a script, the most they will stick their neck out with is a 'CONSIDER.'

The script I'd submitted had already made it through about ten readers in the Chesterfield Writer's Film Project, so I know it was a good script. On top of that, it received "recommend" from two of the biggest agencies in the city—CAA and William Morris, both of which called it "strong and compelling."

The reader at Broder-Kurland, however, saw it as a "confusing mess." And it must have confused him pretty good because his coverage named characters that didn't even exist in my script, got other characters' names mixed up, summarized the plot incorrectly, and even named the wrong cities for the setting. In short, he didn't read it—or he only half-read it. Regardless, he was paid his $50 reader's fee. Maybe he wasn't talented. Maybe he was jaded. Maybe it wasn't interesting enough to him to keep him alert or it was his tenth script that day and they all ran together in his mind. Maybe it couldn't star Julia Roberts?

All I can say is don't take the reader's opinion too seriously either way. In most cases, the person covering your script has no more experience or knowledge than you do. Remember they come with their own prejudices.

If you're able to get a copy of your coverage, read it through and consider whether the reader has made valid criticisms that need to be changed. If so, change the script before resubmitting it. But if it's obvious that the reader was unfocused or had another agenda or just didn't get your style, let it go and move on. There's a reason there are hundreds of channels on TV to choose from—not everyone likes the same shows. And not everyone will like what you write.

Back to agents: I eventually got one. How is a story in itself. I got a bunch of rejections. The producers were taking their time coming up with the $10,000 I asked them for at Le Petit Four on the Sunset Strip. I was feeling a bit desperate.

In the wake of 9/11, the action script I'd written about government operatives who become clandestine terrorists on behalf of the oil industry and bomb the Capital during the State of the Union Address was no longer as appealing as it had been when I had moved here twelve days before September 11th. Especially since the story ended with the space shuttle crashing into a building. It was all just a bit too prescient. It even had Arnold Schwarzenegger as the Governor of California (three years before he ran) and Republicans trying to change the Constitution so he could become President. Freaky prescient. The lawyer I mentioned told me to put it away for five years and not to even bother trying to sell it. So I had to switch gears.

The whole country was depressed. I was feeling stupid for selling my all my stuff and moving here, and I was watching Oprah as she continued to tell people to follow their bliss. I had this idea about a guy whose life falls apart because he follows Oprah's advice. Then I changed it to his life falls apart because the women in his life follow Oprah's advice. I called it *Oprah Winfrey Hates My Guts*.

Remember when I said that everyone knows someone? Well, everyone swears they know Oprah, or someone who works for Oprah. In this case, it was my lawyer's secretary. She insisted I meet her at the Big Boy on Riverside in Burbank on Saturday morning. I went with my wife and child. She was there with her friends and her pregnant daughter.

One of these friends swore she knew someone who worked for Oprah and the secretary took my script and said she would give it to her. They all laughed out loud at the title. I never heard about it again.

At that same time the secretary told me that she could send my other scripts out to prodcos instead of agents if I wanted, and save me the money. Of course I did.

The whole point of getting an agent is to get them to send your stuff to prodcos. (Deals are fairly standard nowadays, so it's not like they do much negotiating). If she could mail out scripts, I didn't think I'd even need an agent. Besides, copying scripts cost about $3 each and mailing is another $4. She said to send her a list of everyone I wanted to send it to. Cool. I did.

She didn't send them out.

About three months later, she still hadn't sent out a single script. I called and told her I could send them myself, using the attorney's return address and a letter on his letterhead. I sent her a copy of the letter I intended to send. She repeated she would send them, but she'd just been busy.

A month later she *still* hadn't sent them. So I did what I had said I would. I sent them under the attorney's letterhead (copied easily enough with a computer), and under his name but not his signature. I put my initials instead—you know, like when someone dictates a letter?

For the second time in my life, the shit hit the fan. A few days later, I got a call from the secretary, "T.R., did you send out scripts under Benny's (not his real name) letterhead?"

"Yes."

"Oh my God, what possessed you to do that?"

"I told you I was going to do it. You didn't seem to have time. I sent you a copy of the letter."

"I never told you you could do that. Benny is furious."

"Well, let me speak to him." She said she'd call me back, and about one minute later she did. She had Benny on the phone.

Benny asked the same question. I explained the reason and how I'd waited four months for the secretary to do it. How I'd sent her a copy of the letter I planned to send. And figured it must have been okay since she didn't say no.

"On a scale of one to ten, in terms of anger, I'm about a thirteen right now. I'm trying to run a business here. You can't do this. I have a reputation. I need the list of everyone you sent this to. I need that list an hour ago!"

"No problem." I sent the list along with a letter in which I joked that I knew he was a negotiator and that if he said he was a thirteen, he was probably only a six or seven.

Benny called me back. Said I was nuts. I asked him how he found out I'd sent the script out.

"I got a call this morning from the president of Universal telling me she read the script I sent her. I told her, I didn't send you any script. She said, 'That's funny, I have a letter in my hand on your letterhead asking me to read this script by T.R. Locke.' I said, 'Well, I didn't send you any script.' She said, 'Well, it's very good.' So I said, 'Well, I do know T.R..' She said she'd be willing to make it if it was packaged."

"Damn, Mary Parent liked my script?!"

"Yeah, she did, asshole. So did Amy Baer over at Columbia. But listen, don't ever do any crap like this again. I mean…if I were to send a script, I certainly wouldn't send it to the president of production at a studio. My God, are you an idiot? Look, you lucked out this time. Is this list complete?"

"Yeah."

"Good. Good luck. And by the way, Jeremy Kleiner over at The Donners' Company wants to see it. Send me a copy of the script."

"What do you mean he wants to see it? How'd he hear about it?"

"It's making the rounds of the young turks. You're on their radar. Tom Lassally over at Giant Robot wants you to go see him in Santa Monica."

I go meet Tom Lassally. He was running a production/management company called Giant Robot above the Promenade. I'm not sure why producers are so often managers, but probably just to get more money out of the talent. I met with him and two other members of the company, Robin and David.

Tom told me he used to be a VP at Warner Bros. and was on his own now. He was working on an *American Idol*-like television show that was geared towards finding the next president of the United States.

I didn't get the concept because I figured anyone who could possibly be a serious contender for the White House wouldn't have time to be on a weekly TV show. But I wasn't a former VP at Warner's so what did I know? He also told me that he was buying a stake in the WWF or some wrestling federation—now that was cool.

Anyway, I asked how they'd heard about me. David said that he'd gotten the script from someone over at DreamWorks and that DreamWorks loved it. I hadn't heard that. But from the excitement beaming off these guys, something was going on. It was weird. I was excited. They wanted to manage me. They were very tight about their clients and only managed the best and they believed I could be one of them—so they said. Wow. We talked about my other ideas—they loved the action script. They liked the Oprah thing more. Everything was amazing. I was amped.

Finally, they told me that Damon Dash from Roc-A-Fella Productions (Jay-Z's company) was looking for a script like this one and they wanted my permission to send it over to him. They said Damon had a ton of money and would throw it at this in a heartbeat. Of course it was all good to me. They wanted me to send over my other scripts so they could go to work advising me on them, getting me ready to blow up with their great management. I sent everything. I was on cloud nine.

I went home and looked up Tom Lassally online. Impressive. I gained a new level of respect for him. Here's an excerpt from my journal:

I looked up Tom Lassally on Google and found all this information about him being associated with the best in the industry. Suddenly now I'm scared. I've got this feeling of needing to be more impressive. I've always felt myself to be a fairly successful man, but when I meet these people out here, it really seems like I have no idea what money is.

Tom had a friend named Jay Maloney, who was a protégé of Michael Ovitz of CAA. This guy was huge before he was even thirty—repping people like Spielberg and Letterman. But shortly after turning 35 he killed himself—hung himself by a belt in the bathroom of his house. He was a cocaine addict and at one point Mike Ovitz, the president of Columbia, Tom Lassally and someone else went to him to do an intervention that didn't work.

Tom is mentioned in the same chapter of The Big Deal as Alan Gasmer. It's really weird. Tom was one of the buyers at Warner Brothers and he was the guy trying to reach Bruce Berman, then pres of WB, now head of Village Roadshow, stuck on the tarmac at JFK. How weird is that? Berman said if Tom had reached him and they'd gotten the script, they would have made the movie [some magician spec script, I think, which another studio bought for several million dollars]. I guess what's got me excited is that the same guy who liked that script likes Prophets and Kings. I'm really hoping it means something.

When I think of people who make millions of dollars it just impresses the hell out of me. I've always wanted that but have not yet been able to get it. Here's a guy who hangs out with his buddies in Africa rafting down the Zambezi River. I can't even imagine that. Not only having enough money to go to Africa with your friends, but to do it just for the rafting? Not that I'd do that—God knows I can think of a million other things to do with

> *my money in Africa. But as far as traveling for water sports, the*
> *best I could do is a pontoon for a weekend at the Dells.*

Alas, I never heard from Tom Lassally or Giant Robot again.

I later found out that Damon Dash didn't want the script. He wanted a vanity script that he could star in instead. Apparently, the only reason they were so hot on me was because they thought they could make a quick buck with Damon. Once he was out of the picture, I was too. What about all that stuff they said? I don't know. I don't know why people act like that, but that may explain why stars don't consider anything unless it comes with a check.

It seems to me that fake, over-the-top enthusiasm and flattery is the lube Hollywood uses so they can stick it in you easier. Stars know this, so their agents cut through the flattery and won't let a star look at anything that doesn't have cash attached—meaning the producers already have the money to produce the film and the actor will be paid for his time. If there's no money ready to be paid to the actor, the agent usually dumps the script. After all, the actor's time is the agent's money. Why should he allow his client to look at a new writer's script when there's no guaranteed payday behind it? In the agent's mind, there are plenty of good scripts for the actor to choose from, the actor doesn't need to waste time (thus the agent's money) on an unsure thing. And even with sure things, agents guarantee their star clients get paid by having them sign pay or play contracts.[5]

This reality presents another catch-22, which is that studios won't finance films without stars, but stars won't read a script that doesn't have the cash attached. That's just one more thing that makes breaking into Hollywood so difficult.

Jeremy Kleiner was the other person my attorney said wanted to meet me. Jeremy was an assistant for Richard Donner (*Lethal Weapon*, etc.) and

---

5   A **pay or play** *clause (or guaranteed contract) in an entertainment contract means that the person who is being hired (typically an actor) is guaranteed payment regardless of whether he or she actually works. For example, if a natural disaster shuts down a production, or a new director is brought on who wants to make casting changes, actors with pay-or-play contracts will receive their contracted salary even though they are no longer on the project.*

his wife, Lauren Schuler Donner (producer of the *X-Men* among others) at The Donners' Company. I was super impressed because Richard Donner not only directed that amazing *Twilight Zone* starting William Shatner with the teddy bear/gremlin thingy on the plane's wing during the rain storm (the best *Twilight Zone* ever), but he also used to direct the *Banana Splits*, which I loved as a child. And he directed episodes of my all-time favorite childhood show, *The Six Million Dollar Man*. Did I mention the Chris Reeves *Superman* movies? *The Omen* trilogy? His bio is remarkable and dates back to 1960.

Anyway, Jeremy called me up and said he loved my script and liked to keep up with all the new writers in town. He said that he knew some people he wanted to send it to and would I mind? Of course I wouldn't mind. One of the people he sent it to was Peter Heller.

Peter had produced two movies I loved, *Like Mike* and *Brown Sugar*. He'd also produced Snoop Dogg's first movie, *Bones*, which I wasn't so hot on. And he produced a flick called *Caught Up* with Bokeem Woodbine—it was decent. Peter called and said he liked my writing and we talked. By the end of the convo, he said he wanted to rep me as a manager. I was on my way.

Peter advised me on some edits and then he sent it to a few agent friends of his. One was Sandy Weinberg of Summit Talent and Literary Agency. Sandy had me in to talk and said he believed he could sell me. He told me he wanted to sign me. But later, I realized that what he actually did was "hip pocket" me. Meaning, he tied me up without formal papers. Benny kept asking for the paperwork. Sandy never sent it, but he would send me out and he would send my script out, but always, "first, there would need to be some changes."

It's important to realize that an agent specializes in selling. When an agent advises you to change your script, he's doing it purely from a marketing standpoint. He knows that certain prodcos or execs are looking for particular types of projects. He's telling you to make changes to get you to fit your script to those known interests.

That's what Sandy was doing with my script. He wanted to change it because, in his opinion, my script straddled two markets and as he put it, "The people who would want to make it for the violence of it wouldn't like the intelligence of it (Damon and Roc-A-Fella), and the people who would want to make it for its intelligent message, wouldn't like the violence."

"But it reflects the complexity of the real world."

"Doesn't matter. It starts violent. The people who want violence will read it and get upset that the violence doesn't continue. The people who want an intelligent story won't read past the first violent scene."

Welcome to Hollywood. Apparently, it didn't matter that the presidents of production of two of the biggest studios said they'd do it if it were packaged. No prodco would put the package together because they wouldn't even finish reading it—unlike all these folks who loved it. Or did they not really love it? I was starting to get confused.

Don't you market a script like this by saying, "Universal and Columbia are willing to do it if you package it?" Duh? I guess not.

I didn't know anything then. I thought studios make movies. They don't. They finance them.

Prodcos make movies. They get the stars "attached," and the director and the script and producer, and they take the whole "package" over to the studio and the studio agrees to finance and distribute the film if the numbers and the players look right. *Voila.* Nothing like I thought before I got here. But that explains why you always see some big studio name at the beginning of movies and other companies' names afterwards.

The problem with what agents think prodcos want is that what prodcos want changes every Monday morning with the revelation of the weekend box office numbers. Everyone in Hollywood is looking for something similar to whatever just made $100M over the weekend. So your agent's advice can change just as frequently.

The second, more important problem is that you can lose your mind trying to please your agent. Agents aren't writers—none of them are. Most of them are former execs or producers—they are lawyers with connections for marketing. What's important for you is to write what's in your heart and try to address the main issues the agent suggests, if you can. Meanwhile, keep your scripts ready for when something similar becomes a hit. And yes, that means when you pitch your story and then later read that a studio somewhere is developing your story, or releasing it in theaters, get your script ready to go out if the film does good box office. Yes it's stupid, but that's how things work here.

The best example of what Hollywood power players are like are political pundits on TV. Before a race, they tell you who's going to win what state and why. After people vote and pundits are proven wrong, they tell you they didn't say what they said and why what happened happened. We keep watching and they keep their jobs even though it's apparent to the whole world they have no idea what they're talking about. Stock market reporters do the exact same thing.

Agents and managers pretend to know things. They pretend to understand the world well enough to prognosticate with the best of them. The problem is that the best of them aren't very good. Remember, an agent is guessing at what will make your script sell. What he really means is that he thinks he's guessing right; and he thinks it so much that he won't be able to muster up the confidence to send your script out and risk his reputation as a finder of talent unless you make the changes he thinks are necessary.

Sometimes they are right. Most times they are wrong. Either way, you want them working hard, so unless you're willing to walk away from your agent, do as much as you can to keep him positive about you.

The title of this WIK indicates that these "percenters" are overrated, but I don't mean they are useless. Nor do I mean they aren't necessary in some ways.

The main role of an agent is to know who's doing what and to try to get you before the right people so they can sell you. The main job of a publicist is to get you known and have your material, or at least your name, seen by many. The main job of an attorney is to make sure you're protected legally. The main job of a manager is to help you know who you are and keep you on that track—doing projects that help you reach your goals. So each of these people have their place, although more ways to get your stuff seen, to know what's going on in the industry, and to market your own stuff, particularly via the internet, become available every day.

Larger agencies work like the studios of old. If you're not part of their stable of talent, you won't get hired to work in the movies they help package, so being part of those larger agencies might get you work you couldn't get other places. However, those agencies are so large that they can sometimes lose you too. And forget about personal attention.

Sometimes, when you entrust someone with your dreams, it's easy to think they share the same vision as you. They seem to want what you want. That's not necessarily true. For the most part, the percenters just want the money. And if what you've got isn't selling, they have to deal with someone who is. For them, it's a numbers game.

So remember, no one cares about your career more than you do. Every percenter—be it an agent, manager, lawyer, publicist or whatever new unnecessary attachment is dreamed up in Hollywood—has about forty of you as clients. That fake sincerity you sense is just that—it's not really personal, it's business.

If no agency picks you up, don't let that discourage you. I've even heard of some creative individuals who started their own agency and sent scripts to studios under their own letterhead. There are so many agencies most producers won't know anyway. If they like the script, they won't care.

The point is that it must be a numbers game for you too—meaning you have to keep putting out whatever your product is—if this one doesn't work, maybe the next one will, but whatever you do don't stop because on your road to stardom...

In Hollywood, You Will Face More Rejection Than You Ever Imagined

I t doesn't really matter what you bring to the table, the fact remains that, on any given day, only so many people will be on the same page as you. That simply means that rejection is a major part of eventually reaching your goal.

As I said about dealing with percenters, success in Hollywood is essentially a numbers game. The more people you meet, the more auditions you go on, the more scripts you write, the more times you call, the more letters you write, the better your chance of eventual success.

You need to develop a thick skin. Huge stars who've already made their names still sometimes languish for years trying to get a project made. Their ideas are rejected or shelved. They, like you, wait for their chance. In the meantime, they deal with the rejection.

Even some at the top of their careers find themselves limited in their ability to express their artistic views.

No doubt stars resent being trapped in the bubble of their type. Many try to break out, but they find the public doesn't accept them when they do. If they push too hard, many struggle with keeping their audience.

Studios struggle with the costs of films and the fact that, as William Goldman says, "Nobody knows anything."

The risk involved in seriously promoting any venture is considerable. Not only that, but the very nature of artistic expression is subjective. The key is whether or not people will get you and whether Hollywood can make money off of your artistic expression.

The reason so many songs sound alike and so many movies are alike is because somewhere that "type" of song or movie or artistic expression succeeded.

My daughter could tell the plots of movies she'd never seen by the time she was seven. She said they were all alike with different names—and she was right. But Hollywood made money on that type before, and that's their basis for believing they will make money on it again.

That's the whole justification for the star system. People attach to a familiar face. Once that attachment is made, it's hard to see that actor without experiencing some of what that actor did before. For instance, I can't see Eddie Murphy's face without laughing. Many can't. That's why he can't play dramatic roles. His curse is that he is so funny. If he were less funny, he might pull it off. But again, he came to Hollywood as a comedian and has been hired to play his comedic personas ever since.

For instance, Will Smith and Tom Hanks (both originally TV comedic stars) are the only two actors that come to mind who I would buy in either a silly comedy or a serious drama. Jim Carrey, another comedian, tries very hard, but people still don't buy him as serious. But neither Tom Hanks nor Will Smith are as funny as Eddie Murphy. Jim Carrey *was*—thus Jim Carrey's problem transitioning. Still, people flock to see him in a comedy, but apart from *Eternal Sunshine of the Spotless Mind* (which I thought was kind of funny until the end), his dramas basically go straight to DVD.

I think Will Smith gets away with being accepted in different genres because he plays semi-funny characters in all his movies. He is eternally the wisecracking, nice black guy. So his characters always border on both dramatic and comedic anyway. He's in a lucky niche.

I once heard Will Smith say that if he's cast in a movie, he brings an automatic audience of twenty-five million black people. That may not be true, but it's obvious that a lot of filmmakers believe that about him, and he certainly knows how to market himself.

And ultimately, that's what it's all about. As an artist in Hollywood, you must convince someone that your expression will sell to millions. Having to work to get executives and producers to believe that—to overcome their own doubts and fears—is what prolongs the time to reach success in Hollywood.

Some people reject you with kindness. "We loved it, but it's not the type of film we're looking to make now." "Great audition, I was pulling for you, but the company decided on someone else. I hope to work with you some day."

Most just blow you off: "Thank you. Next." "No thank you." "Pass." Or worst of all, no response at all.

I certainly appreciate the kind words of encouragement concerning my talent. It's kind of like a woman saying, "You're cute, but I'm married. Sorry."

The blow-offs are like a woman turning away in the middle of your introduction. I tend to want to know what happened. Was it my breath?

I've come to realize that I'll never know the answer. The answer actually doesn't matter. All that matters is that I move on. There's no sense in prophesying the regrets she will have for turning me down. And at least she was forthright. She's obviously not interested.

The worst to me are the never-responders. I take that back. It's not the worst to not respond. The worst is to respond enthusiastically at first, then disappear.

I have this theory I call "The Emotional Gap Theory." What it essentially states is that the level of emotion you experience in any given situation is a function of the level of emotion you were experiencing just prior to that event.

For instance, when I was just out of high school, I had a job working the morning shift at McDonald's. Perhaps the most outrageous aspect of this employment was the requirement the manager placed on us to be at the store by 5 a.m., but not to punch in until 6 a.m. As far as I know, that practice was outlawed in 1865. But, if I arrived at the store, which was some fifteen miles from my home, even five minutes past 5 a.m., I would not be allowed in the store. I would have to go back home and miss that day's work. And missing that day's work was then written on my record and I was issued a warning. Three warnings and I would be suspended for three days from work. My God, the things you put up with when you're young and broke.

The other outrageous aspect of this job was the clocking of precisely thirty-nine hours per week. At forty hours a week, you were considered a full-time employee and would be entitled to particular benefits by law, the main benefit being health insurance. No one except managers and crew chiefs ever were paid benefits.

But the worst part was that the hours were calculated bi-weekly— that is, we were only required to stay below 80 hours for every two-week period. In many situations, I found myself working a sixty-hour week one week, then only a nineteen-hour week the next week. Up at 3 a.m., back home by 6 or 7 p.m. on some days.

I worked the back drive-thru window. My entire day consisted of hearing a buzz in my headset and saying, "Welcome to McDonald's. May I take your order?"

I remember my phone would ring at home and I would answer it, "Welcome to McDonald's..." People thought it was funny, but it was hell.

I hated the entire two months I lasted at that job. The only joy I had during that time were Friday nights with friends at a restaurant called Geraci's in Cleveland Heights. I couldn't wait for Friday nights. When I look back on those memories of Geraci's it seems as if I approached nirvana. They rank as some of the happiest days of my life.

When I finally left for college, my friends and I would return to the restaurant during trips home. I wanted to capture a hint of the joy I remembered. We had a great time, but it was nothing like it was when I worked at McDonald's. I later put together that it wasn't that anything changed in my friendships or in the quality of Geraci's. What changed was that I was no longer miserable in my daily life before I got to Geraci's, so the joy of conversation and pizza with my friends was not perceived as amazing. That's my gap theory.

If you touch a cold pipe and then touch a warm one, your hand feels the sensation of burning as if you'd touched a red-hot pipe. The sensation is caused by the difference in the temperature the hand experiences—the temperature gap from very cold to suddenly warm is similar to the gap from normal body temperature to burning hot, so your body reacts the same.

As far as rejection in Hollywood goes, one of the most painful kinds is the one that comes after you've told all your friends and family you booked the TV show and find out the producers went with someone else. The gap that opens between your joy and your disappointment is tremendous.

For me, perhaps the most painful rejection is being offered a contract and having it fail to materialize. I've already spent the money in my mind. I have to retire my fantasies. And if no excuse is offered on top of that, it's just debilitating.

The point of this thing I WIK is just to expect rejection or disappointment sometimes, and keep pressing on. Remember that rejection is part of the game and don't take it personally.

For actors, this can be very hard. Actors stand in front of someone face-to-face. They often get to see someone's reaction. They may be told to try the lines different ways and then be dismissed without a word. They may be called back again and again and still not book the gig. Actors must be able to let it go and move on.

Writers have a different pain. Some writers come to Hollywood with original ideas they want to sell. Others come with sample scripts of other TV shows they simply want to contribute to. Both types come with talent.

The writer with the original vision, however, faces judgment beyond his technical skills. The original writer may be an amazing technician, but it won't matter if no one catches his vision and he's not interested in writing other people's ideas. The rejection of an original script—especially one dear to a writer's heart, and which he may have nurtured for years—is deeper than the rejection one faces trying to be a part of someone else's vision.

One is like getting a job working for someone else. If you don't get this job, you go for the next. The other is like starting your very own business. But if your business fails to attract investment capital after years of dreaming and working hard to develop the plan... ouch.

Original writers, therefore, need to approach Hollywood with the understanding that everything here is done in collaboration—many, many people must share your vision for it to become a reality here.

Even stories that everyone has already agreed to film can fall apart for any reason. Original writers need to keep their minds open to other ways of communicating their story. Will it work as a book? Will it work as a stage play? Can it be filmed independently?

Having alternative routes to your vision reaching the public is key to maintaining your power in this industry notorious for discounting the contributions of writers.

The WGA strike of 2007-2008 recently came to an end. For a while there, Hollywood went into full-scale panic. People were laid off, having had no idea their jobs were tied to writers writing. Actors didn't act. Directors didn't direct. Makeup artists had no one to put makeup on. It was pretty ugly...literally.

So never underestimate the power of an original story. *Star Wars* was just a story.

I have a screen capture from *The Making of Star Wars* DVD. In it, George Lucas sits at his desk with a three-ring binder of paper and scribbles, "*Star Wars*—Episode II." He flips a page and writes, "Fade in," skips a line, and writes, "Space." The rest is history—His Story. The original writer's story holds that same seed of promise.

And, as I mentioned before, every major studio in Hollywood rejected *Star Wars*. If that's not encouraging, I don't know what is.

The rejection of a story does not mean the story is not valuable. It merely means you haven't sold the vision yet. Keep selling and if you're an actor, keep auditioning because...

Hollywood Has as Many "Used-To-Bes" as Wannabes

N otice I called them "used-to-bes", not "has-beens." All I mean is that there are many people here who used to be much bigger than they are now. They are often still very impressive, but not on the level they were at one time.

I wrote earlier about meeting so many people on their way down. It's a fine line between being "on your way down" and "trying to get back into the game." Because it's always about marketing, people who made it once must continue to make it to stay on top here. Celebrities who don't may become "one-hit wonders" or, if they're lucky, reprocessed reality show contestants, if not security guards and ticket takers.

If you're not a celebrity though, you may just end up back at the job you left. There are tons of writers, actors, comedians, dancers, etc., who achieve a little success. They write for a show for a season. They even star in minor parts on TV and movies. You may recognize them sometimes, but they aren't stars. Such people make up the mosaic of Los Angeles.

They aren't rich. Many are just barely hanging on. They may have been big once, but not any more.

It's truly amazing how fast money can be spent here. We read about the outlandish salaries people are paid here, but we don't realize the uncertainty of their continued success. An actor can fall out of popularity as easily as he fell into it. The stress takes its toll.

Professional athletes have a similar situation. They are paid outlandish salaries, but they may injure themselves and never make another dime off their athletics.

When I was twenty years old and living in Cleveland, I took a licensing course to sell life insurance. In my class was Mike Pruitt, star of the Cleveland Browns. He'd recently retired and was beginning his new career in the insurance business. Although he may enjoy a generous pension from the NFL, no doubt it's a considerable cut in pay from his playing income. The same thing can happen to Hollywood stars.

As a mortgage broker here in L.A., I've been privy to a good number of celebrity clients' personal financial information—tax returns, bank statements, retirement statements, etc. Income for most of them varies wildly by year depending on what projects they were working on.

Absolutely alarming, though, are the fees so many pay to their management (20%), lawyers (10%), accountants (10%), agents (10%), publicists (5%) (that's 55% already!), stock brokers, caregivers, nannies, drivers—their people, and the money they pay to taxes. Even though I've seen some accountants do things with numbers that border on preposterous to limit the taxes their clients pay, it's still a huge chunk of income eaten up before they see a dime.

For the people who find themselves on this level of success and living the lifestyle that accompanies it, the need to keep earning staggering amounts of money becomes paramount.

The lucky few who can continue to generate that income regularly, do fine. But for many, and possibly most, the lush life doesn't last always.

In fact, many newer celebs find themselves broke or bankrupted before they've even blown up. Will Smith reported that for the first few years of his starring on *Fresh Prince of Bel Air,* he wasn't making anything because he was paying back taxes to the IRS from his days as a rapper. How many rappers have that tax experience without having the bailout of a hit TV series?

Answer: Lots of them. So it's important that their next album be a hit, too.

The music business is particularly tricky because so much usually goes into developing an artist that the artists can find themselves in actual debt to their label for years after their album comes out.

What you see on MTV, VH1, and BET may look glamorous, but it's all rented for the day, just for the image. Don't be fooled by it.

In fact, more than one celebrity client of mine had no idea how much money they even had. They were simply given allowances by their accountants. Why? Because they'd been irresponsible with their spending and gotten in over their heads in the past. Coming to Hollywood looking for the type of glamour you see on TV could land you in the same position.

It may sound cool to refer someone to your accountant when you're ready to buy a house, but having an accountant who knows where all your money is when you don't know is just asking for embezzlement. And it's really interesting when your accountant tells your broker you can't afford the house you're trying to buy, but won't tell you.

Oprah says she learned the hard way to sign all her checks herself. I wonder how many millions have been stolen from her? Oprah's not hurting—she's perennially on top of the game, but many others aren't so lucky.

If you're fortunate enough to make it, make sure you mind your money. A single payday here can retire you for a decent lifetime in another part of the country, or might only last you a couple of years in L.A.

Remember, too, the main point of this WIK: Just because you make it once, doesn't mean you'll keep it going. There is a constant need to produce and keep producing once you get inside the business. Your agent will constantly be looking for the next thing you do so he can keep selling you.

One of the harshest realities for me to face after I got my agent was that he was never as focused on my original script as I was. He saw that script as having gotten me in the door and possibly one day being produced. But once he sent it out, and I took a few meetings on it, it did what it did and then he was ready to move on. I still wanted to see my movie made. I labored over that script for years and I fully intended it to become a movie, not a calling card. He wanted my next script, but I wanted him to sell the one he had.

I wish I had known that's not quite how it works. I was looking for validation. The fact that my script had not been made caused me to doubt my talent. I wrote new stuff, but I kept wondering if I could top what I'd already done. And if that script hadn't sold, was there a chance for anything else? The only way to find out is to keep writing.

Stay on top of your game if you want a serious career because, oddly enough...

You Can Be in Films, Commercials, Movies, and/or TV Shows and Never Be Seen By Anyone

I wish I'd known this before I told everyone back home to be looking for me, but less than fifty percent of my nationwide commercials have ever aired.

Before I came to Hollywood, I never realized that it's actually possible to make a bunch of commercials or be in a number of films and yet never be seen. But extras can make a fairly decent living and appear in tons of movies without the camera ever catching their faces.

When my wife first decided to start doing some acting, she booked a lot of extra work through Central Casting here in Burbank. Extras show up early in the morning along with the rest of the crew, and they stay on set all day during filming. They are the background people in every movie.

My wife has been in episodes of *ER*, *CSI* and *Strong Medicine*. She's also been in the *Italian Job* and *The Incredible Hulk* and a dozen other films. If there's a cool part to doing extra work, it's that you get to hang out on sets and see and sometimes talk to stars and directors and understand a bit of how movie making works.

I sat with my daughter once when she served as an extra in *Legally Blonde 2*. I was bored out of my mind. I have never found film sets to be as interesting as so many others do. I even got bored watching them film chase scenes and shootouts in Chicago. Being on a set doesn't do it for me. But it's good work for many people in L.A. It requires no particular skills except that you show up on time and have certain types of clothes to wear.

I remember one twenty-year-old actor telling me that he made $50K a year doing extra work, just on weekends. He said he was a SAG member— SAG members get paid twice as much for extra work. But they also get overtime and weekend pay. Because he only worked weekends, he was always being double- and triple-paid so that it worked out to $1,000 a week. I just remembered that story, and I could really use the money now. Maybe I should look into that. His secret was looking sixteen—I can't quite pull that off. He was in tons of music videos and teen TV shows and movies.

But if you want to give extra work a try, show up in Hollywood, jump over the hill to Burbank, and sign up with Central Casting. They take your photo and get some info about you, including special skills—anything from the ability to ride a motorcycle or windsurf, to willingness to eat bugs or work naked.

Next, go home and call Central Casting every day. You will hear a voice recording telling you what they're looking for. If you fit, call back. If you're lucky—which usually just means calling in fast enough—they'll book you for the gig.

Show up on time and ready to work and you'll do fine. The checks go to Central Casting and they pay you via Entertainment Partners or some other payroll service. On the sets, you can make friends with other actors, learn about other gigs and learn the tricks of the trade—such as how to get a SAG card to double your pay and get benefits, how to land better auditions, and possibly even find an agent.

If you're not the talk-to-strangers type, bring something to read or do. There's a lot of down time on a set. You might be thrilled the first couple hours, but unless you're mentally challenged or really into how movies, commercials or TV shows are made, it will get old fast. That's pretty much all there is to being an extra.

BTW, there are whole books out there that tell you how to become a working actor in Hollywood that boil down to nothing more than what I just told you in the last six paragraphs.

The commercials I mentioned doing at the beginning of this chapter were not extra jobs. They were featured commercials. I auditioned. I was called back. I was picked. I was measured and outfitted with new purchased wardrobes. I had my makeup done. I had my time to be on set and the camera was right in my face the whole time. Yet the commercials never aired. I was paid, but I've never seen them on television. And they won't release copies of them for me to have until they actually air, so I can't even prove to anyone that they actually happened. But every year, I get checks to renew the commercials—just in case the clients decide to use them.

One of the commercials I remember that never aired was for Papa John's Pizza. There must have been thirty actors called to the beach pavilion in San Pedro. I played one of four construction workers. We had brand new clothes and boots that the wardrobe mistress and her assistant ripped and dirtied to make us look less like actors and more like real construction workers. She ground the new tan leather boots into the flowerbed, scratched them up with a rasp and beat them with a rock even though the camera never went anywhere near our feet.

The lighting crew took a giant white silkscreen and blocked the real sun, then set up an artificial sun to shine down on us.

We ate tons of Papa John's pizza with different toppings. Each shot had to be of us taking the first bite—not a second bite. We had to tear it from a brand new pizza each time, too. There must have been eight different types of pizza. We could only eat one bite of each piece, which had to be piping hot so you could see the steam. And they filmed us from every possible angle—beneath us, above us, past this guy's shoulder, under this guy's arm, box passed over, box passed under, box dropped out of scene.

All the pizza wouldn't have been so bad if we weren't the first group to shoot that morning. We'd just finished eating made-to-order omelets that were so tasty that I had had two. (One of the perks of most paid acting gigs is the food service provided by the production company. The purpose of providing the food service is to keep actors around so as not to have to wait for them to return from lunch, snacks, etc. You can eat all you want and there's usually a surprising variety—including sticks of gum and assorted candy bars.)

There were only four of us in the construction scene, which meant four bites from each pizza; then the rest of it was tossed in the trash. We must have gone through twenty boxes of pizza. The thing that took the most time was reheating the pizzas so they were piping hot.

The rest of the twenty-six actors were waiting for their turn as a school band, a group of dance students, and a few other set-ups. I'm glad we went first. They must have been there all night. But none of that commercial was ever shown on television.

But that's just the commercials. What's really wild is that tons of movies sit in cans and are never released. Many studio films never see the light of a projector or a TV set. Actors act, writers write, directors direct, composers compose, musicians play and... *poof.* Nothing. It's one thing in Hollywood to make a movie. It's quite another to get it distributed either to theaters or on DVD.

You can make your film independently, spend all your savings and your family's money, and still no one ever see it. Each year, thousands of completed films are submitted to hundreds of film festivals around the world. Most of them never get accepted. Even the ones that do, and that generate some buzz, rarely see a normal release to a wide audience— showing only in art theaters in major cities on certain days. I'm sure that's not the dream the filmmakers had in mind when they set out to make a movie.

But even in films that get made and released, actors often find their entire scene has been cut from the movie—determined to be unnecessary by post editors. Can you imagine actually being in a huge movie, doing a big part and telling everyone about it only to find it not in the movie when it comes out? Ugh. Some don't even make the deleted scenes section of the DVD.

So make sure your film, commercial, CD or whatever is actually coming out or airing before you tell everyone. But if you are seen on TV or in a movie, you will do well to remember this next thing I wish I knew...

Folk Back Home Will Think You're Money Even When You're Broke

If they see you on TV, they will think you're a millionaire. There will be no convincing your family or friends back home that you don't have money once you're on television.

For some reason, people believe bizarre things about salaries for actors. Everyone hears what movie stars make and they assume most actors share the same wealth. Wrong. Most actors are poor and must work elsewhere to make ends meet.

California by itself has that vibe. People back home already tend to think you're a big baller just because you live here. The fact that you share an apartment with two other apartment mates and you're all struggling just to get the rent in before the landlord calls just doesn't ring true to folks outside—not if you've ever been on TV.

I think something happens when people outside the industry see you on television. It was recently reported that the cast members of *Grey's*

Anatomy, due to it being such a huge hit, are now being paid $250,000 per episode. That's an amazing salary. But when people hear that number and then see your commercial come on during *Grey's Anatomy...voila*! In their minds, you too make $250,000 a week.

You may need to nip that in the bud before someone back in Trenton kidnaps your momma.

Someone You Know, Who Came Here Years After You, Will Get a Movie Made Before You (Inside a Year Or So) and Make It Look Easy

H er name was Karyn Beach. She came to my screenwriting group two years after a friend and I started it. It was my third year in Hollywood.

Karyn was cool. She was from Beachwood, Ohio, just up the road from where I grew up. She was a good writer. She met with the group for about a year.

At the time, I was the only member with an agent and manager and regular meetings at studios. Others in the group had made spec films, placed in writers workshops and writing contests. Karyn had none of these credentials.

She had gotten into a mentoring program through Film Independent's Project Involve. One assignment was to create a short story film script. Karyn had the brilliant idea to write about the soldiers whose job it was to notify next of kin that their loved one had died in service. The short was called *P.N.O.K.—Primary Next Of Kin.*

Within a couple months, Karen had written the 19-page script. Her mentor Carolyn McDonald used to work with Danny Glover's production company. She got the script to Danny and a couple months later, Danny Glover was starring in her film. A few months later, it premiered. Yeah, that quickly.

I was invited to the premier along with the other writers in the group. The theater on the Raleigh Studios lot was packed. What struck me most was that Tiny Lister, Deebo from the movie *Friday*, had to stand against the wall along with others because there were no seats.

It was impressive. The lights dimmed and the film rolled. Karen's name popped up in the credits and we all cheered. We were all happy for her. We were all green with envy, but we were all happy for her.

Karyn was only paid $500 for her writing on the script, but she'd done it. The film played at a few festivals. Although it starred Danny Glover, was well written and it had a few meetings with cable broadcasters, it never got picked up.

Karyn had the great fortune of touching on a subject that many people felt passionately about. The Iraq war was just beginning and over 3,500 soldiers had already died, and many understood that the war had nothing to do with terrorism or weapons of mass destruction. Danny Glover felt passionately about that issue and did the movie *gratis*—helping to produce it in fact.

Sometimes success comes immediately. Sometimes it takes years to become an overnight success.

There are many young actors and actresses here who booked their first audition, had a season on TV, and haven't booked another thing for years since.

Likewise, there are a few who booked their first, second, third and so on auditions and have never had a problem working here.

Unfortunately, Karyn's career didn't take off in the movie business after that film. She moved the next year to Charlotte, N.C. Though she still continues to write and work on film projects, her main work is as a success coach. She did her Hollywood thing and is now off to the next adventure.

Part of that new adventure included scoring a place on *Who Wants to Be A Millionaire?* with Meredith Vieira and winning a cool $100K, of which, she informs me, half went to taxes.

Although Karyn got on that game show in New York after she'd moved to Charlotte, one of the advantages of being in Hollywood is the ability to go on such shows.

A few years back, my wife won a spot on the *Pyramid Game* with Donnie Osmond. She'd advanced to the winner's seat to play for $70,000. The last word for her to advance to the next round was "Coliseum." She drew a blank despite the clues, "Gladiators," "Olympics," and "Stadium." Blank. It happens.

I guess the point here is, just because you get on, it doesn't mean you win. But it's fun to have taken the chance. Likewise, just because you land an agent, doesn't mean everything opens up for you right away. But once you get an agent, remember this next thing I wish I knew...

Don't Fire Your Agent—At Least Not Until You've Secured a Replacement

Yes, I know I said they were overrated, but they still rule most of the world out here. So if you have or get an agent, this advice applies.

I mentioned in the introduction of this book that I'd fired my agent but I never explained what led me to end our relationship. To fire him appeared to be a very sudden decision on my part, even though I'd been thinking about it for some time.

I didn't understand the role of an agent then as I do now. To me, Sandy always seemed to be completely oblivious to the energy it takes to create a screenplay or even a pitch for a screenplay.

I suppose that because he was so used to hearing pitches, he thought stories and ideas popped into writers' heads fully formed. Considerable time and effort is spent putting together coherent and original stories, multi-faceted characters, interesting subplots, twists, and payoffs—especially for a full-length feature film. To me, my agent seemed to simply not "get" the writing process. And it all became a little too frustrating.

I tried to like him, but the more time I spent around him the more fickle I felt he was. "Change the title." "Change the order of events." "Change this... Change that," was always followed by, "If you don't, I can't sell it."

It was all very annoying not only because it was just a matter of his opinion versus mine, but especially because, in a tight script, even a small change in one place necessitates a series of changes throughout the script.

I finally stopped debating and made the decision to fire him after two meetings in particular.

The first was prior to the release of Mel Gibson's *The Passion of the Christ*, when I'd pitched a modern telling of the Biblical story of Elijah as the first superhero. Sandy said, "Nah. Once the world sees *The Passion*, no one will greenlight a religious themed film again. That movie's going to be horrible and die at the box office."

I went back to another pitch meeting with Sandy a few weeks later, after *Passion* had come out to wild unanticipated success, and I pitched a movie called *The Muscle* about a Danny DeVito/Joe Pesci-type character who inherits a trailer park and has to find some muscle to help him run it and it all goes to shit.

Sandy said that it was possibly the best pitch he'd ever heard but that the *Sopranos* had a lock on all the gangster stuff, and Hollywood would never buy another gangster flick. The way he tossed my pitch off showed a complete lack of appreciation for all that went into it. I'd spent weeks formulating that pitch, the characters, the beats of the story. But he blew it off like a stranger, not like an agent—all because he believed *The Sopranos* had cornered the market on all things mobbish.

But that wasn't the worst part. The worst part was what came next. "I really think you should do like I said before and go to work on that Elijah story."

Apart from feeling like I had just walked into the Twilight Zone, I knew right then that this guy would do nothing but annoy and frustrate me. I could see why Joe Eszterhas had brought a hunting knife to a meeting with his agent.

Fortunately for me, I never had to deal with Sandy alone. My manager Peter was always there as a go-between. I would pitch Peter. Peter would make suggestions. I'd make some changes, then pitch him again, and then we'd go together to pitch Sandy. Then I'd go out to the studios or I'd start writing a new project on spec. Peter would read the new script and offer suggestions. I'd make changes. Peter would then send it to Sandy. Sandy would then respond with additional changes or send it out.

Well, once Peter left for Loyola, it took only one phone call with Sandy for me to fire him—the one in which he called to comment on the completed *Elijah* screenplay I'd just spent three months writing.

There was a website called "What's Hot in Hollywood," which tracked the purchasing interest of studios and prodcos. I'd come to realize that Sandy was perusing this site based on the type of scripts or projects he'd suggest I write and the fact that he occasionally wrote articles for the site. The site, however, basically reported that everyone was looking for scripts similar to whatever had been big at the box office the previous weekend.

Passion had been such a huge unexpected hit that for almost three months religious or biblical themed scripts had been listed as "What's Hot." When I'd pitched my *Elijah* story to Sandy a full two months prior to the release of *The Passion* (and I'd not even heard of *The Passion* until Sandy had mentioned it at that pitch meeting) Sandy thought my script was a bad idea. When *Passion* was released and proved there was an audience, suddenly my idea was not only good, but "brilliant" and "great."

Monday morning. Sandy had had my completed script since the previous Wednesday and was due to read it over the weekend. However, that particular Monday morning the "What's Hot" site reported that religious scripts had fallen out of favor due to the sheer abundance of religious themed stories Hollywood had been forced to read and produce immediately after the success of *The Passion*. The site put all "Bible/Religious" themed scripts in the "What's Not" (hot) section.

The phone rang and there was Sandy ranting about how I'd promised him my Elijah script would be an "adventure movie" about Elijah and

Jezebel chasing some McGuffin[6] all over the Middle East like in *The Mummy*.

The hell it was. The pitch was simply this: "Elijah...The Original Superhero—done in the tone of *The Mummy*." It was to be a superhero movie done in the "tone" of *The Mummy*, not the "genre" of *The Mummy*.

"I'm not going to mutilate the Bible and have a holy man, revered by millions, lollygagging about the deserts looking for lost treasure with some skank," I told him. "I was simply going to write about a guy, whom the Bible says traveled in whirlwinds, as the first superhero--a hip story for a modern audience—a huge summer blockbuster for Brad Pitt or Owen Wilson to star."

It seemed wrong to group *The Passion* in the same category as a superhero movie. Would they have done that with *Raiders of the Lost Ark* because the Ark of the Covenant was from the Bible? Or the *Da Vinci Code*?

We argued for an hour. Sandy finally insisted he didn't get it. "I can't sell this."

And I knew it had nothing to do with the fact that I'd written an action movie instead of an adventure movie. I believe he'd read the site that morning—and rather than just tell me that he was afraid he'd missed his window of opportunity to market this script, he tried to put it off on me like I wasn't at the meeting, like I didn't pitch the script, and like I didn't know what the hell I'd pitched.

I decided to check out. "You didn't sell the last one after I made all the changes you suggested." Silence. "You don't sell anything. And, frankly, I'm sick of changing what I'm working on every Monday morning after you read 'What's Hot In Hollywood'."

"Well, maybe you should seek an agent who completely shares your vision." A not-so-veiled threat.

"That's what I was thinking. Thanks for the year and a half. Good luck with your business." And with that, Summit Talent and Literary Agency of Beverly Hills was no longer representing me.

---

6   McGuffin is a term used for an item that drives the action of a film, but is unimportant in itself. Example: The briefcase in **Pulp Fiction**.

No one was.

Still, no one is. No, not because I can't get a literary agent, but because I haven't tried. I've not submitted a single thing to a single entity in two and a half years. Why? Because I was ticked off.

That script was brilliant. Even now, I read it and I cry, laugh out loud and sit jittering with excitement as I turn its pages unable to put it down. And I'm not alone—others respond to it that way as well. The script was good and deserved to be recognized as the story that it was—judged on its own merits, not grouped into a category and dismissed like that.

I looked Sandy Weinberg up to see what he was up to and came across this interview with him at the Hollywood Film Festival, from *Inside Film Magazine Online*, shortly after I'd fired him. Blaustein wrote *Nutty Professor II* and *Coming to America*. I bolded the part I find ironic:

> *Mellot: What is the role for the writer in the writer-agent relationship?*
>
> *WEINBERG: Honesty is absolutely crucial and both sides must know each other's expectations. Also, the writer needs to stay in front of the marketplace. Keep coming up with fresh ideas. Show everyone that you're excited. I think writers should stand tall. A lot of the successful comedy writers are also excellent pitchers.*
>
> *BLAUSTEIN: The only thing I disagree with is about the pitching. Maybe good comedy pitchers should really be comedians. I think the correlation between being a good pitcher and being a good writer is just luck. I don't think a writer should have to worry about being overly entertaining or funny in a pitch. Just be passionate and show that you're very excited about telling your story. Pitching is one of the toughest things to do because you feel like a shoe salesman.*
>
> *WEINBERG: It's also exposing yourself to rejection in its purest form. As writers, to be rejected by someone who's falling asleep or walks out of the room while you're pitching can be devastating.*
>
> *BLAUSTEIN: If you see their eyes rolling back and you have five more minutes to go, you might as well stop. I'm not that*

masochistic to continue that process. Let me just add, that it's very important to get a life outside of this business. Because when things are going well in your career, you're not as wonderful as people tell you and when your career's not going well you're not as bad as they say you are. Don't let what the industry thinks about you determine what you think about yourself. Develop interests outside the industry. Develop a life outside this industry and for god sakes don't marry anyone in the industry. [Audience laughs.]

DEANE: Getting back to the question about what the writer should do in the writer-agent relationship, the most important thing is to keep writing. The agent needs product to sell.

WEINBERG: Don't try to chase the marketplace, because by the time you finish writing for a particular trend, it's passed. Instead develop a distinctive voice by writing what you are passionate about.

That last bit of wisdom is something Sandy learned after our time together. He was chasing the trend created by the *Passion of the Christ* and felt its time had passed, but I'd written what I felt was a great script, regardless of any trend. My script should have gone out. Sandy should have tried to sell it. If not, I should have gotten other representation. But I was at the end of my rope, so instead I got depressed and started down Eszterhas Road.

In the interview above, Blaustein suggested, "Don't let what the industry thinks about you determine what you think about yourself." That's great advice. I think what I did was a little different: I let what I thought about the industry keep me from pursuing my passion.

Unbelievably, I quit writing for two and a half years. The outline for the script I mentioned at the beginning—the one for the producer who'd read that e-mail I wrote to my friends—and this book are the first things I've written since I fired Sandy.

I had gotten so upset and depressed at all the realities I'd uncovered about this business that I felt my writing was in vain. What good was writing if no one would ever read it? What good was the point of meeting after meeting after meeting if the only thing I'd ever get to script would be an episode of *C.S.I.* or *The Omen 6*? What's the point of creating stories if they're only going to get plugged into some pigeonhole and ignored if they're not part of the trend *du jour*?

The point of this WIK is that agents are replaceable. Sure I was angry that I'd spent a year and a half with Sandy and that he came at me the way he did, but his suggestion, whether a real or a veiled threat, that I find an agent that completely shared my view, was on the money. My problem was that I didn't want to search out another agent.

Before I'd found Sandy, I'd felt desperate to get an agent. I didn't want to go back to that. In my rage, I acted too swiftly. It would have been better for me to fire Sandy after I'd found a new agent. I had forgotten a really important lesson I'd learned years ago—the best time to look for a new job is when you've already got one.

Although I spent this entire WIK talking about writing, it applies to music and acting as well. Agents, producers, record execs and managers are notorious for wanting "pets" they can control and command. They want singers to sing in a certain style, actors to act in a certain genre. They are not above telling you that your original song stinks just so they can get you to sing the one they want you to sing instead. Sometimes they're right—listen to what they say and make that decision for yourself. But know that sometimes they're just not looking out for your interests.

Either way, knowing that there are others who may better share your vision and thus better represent you is a good thing. Never give up because someone doesn't get your vision—there's always someone else out there.

Unfortunately, by the time that someone turned up, I'd already given up because...

In Addition to All the Fake Crap, Real Crap Happens, Too

You've read the kind of ridiculousness that happens here in Hollywood, but real genuine problems occur that can be equally frustrating – if not moreso.

One of the harshest realities of Hollywood is the collaborative nature of the work. With the exception of Mel Gibson and Tyler Perry (and a few internet entrepreneurs), no one writes, produces, directs, stars in and distributes their own films or albums or TV shows. This collaborative reality causes tremendous frustration and delays with everything here.

If you take a look at most other industries, there is a product that needs to get to market, and depending on which industry it is, it's pretty much capable of being produced by a single entity.

Let's take cookies. Nabisco wants to make a new cookie. They decide that mint filling in a chocolate cookie might be appealing. How hard is it for Nabisco to produce, distribute and market that new cookie? Not hard at all. It's just a matter of getting the ingredients and the recipe down. The rest is a no-brainer. They already have the cookie marketing and distribution network going.

Before I came to Hollywood, I thought that's how movies were made. As a writer, I basically came up with stories—ingredients for movies. If a studio liked my story, they bought it and made it. In other words, I write. They buy and make. I write the next one, etc. Well, not quite.

There are a lot of arguments about why movies are so expensive to produce—from having to pay stars, to distribution costs, to labor to marketing.

It is rather alarming that, in order to get people to even know that a movie is in theaters, a cost of marketing the movie nearly equivalent to the cost of making the movie is said to be necessary. I'm not sure if that's the reason for the expense or not, but gone are the days of a movie sitting in a theater for weeks until people figure out what it is. It seems movies now have to win on opening weekend or else they're off to DVD the next weekend.

One of the reasons stars are chosen is because the media will give a star free publicity. Talk shows will interview a star and allow them to discuss their new movie, even ask them to. Stars can appear on national awards shows and plug their movies or CDs. Critics will definitely go see a movie with a star in it, and can give it a great review—especially in exchange for an interview. Magazines all vie to be the one with the exclusive cover story on the star with something to sell. It all adds up to free marketing. So stars are paid with that in mind.

In the case of Heath Ledger, a star can even overdose and die and the studio will use it. As the old Hollywood adage goes, "any publicity is good publicity."

I couldn't believe they said that Ledger was so into the dark side of his Joker character that he had to take pills to sleep. That's Hollywood though...made me want to see *The Dark Knight*. I wouldn't be surprised if the next Nicholson movie comes out with a tagline—"Nicholson—so good you have to kill yourself to top him."

It used to be that the cost of printing and distributing hundreds to thousands of reels of film to theaters across the country was one of the biggest expenses of movie-making, and why distribution deals were so important.

Even though distribution can now be done digitally, without the need for printing and shipping film, other production costs are still extravagant. Making movies is expensive and risky. Because of those costs and risks, people involved in making movies like to spread them out as widely as possible.

Studios do this by relegating to the prodcos the responsibility of finding scripts, contracting with directors and actors, and getting that whole group of collaborators together. Prodcos find and develop the story to the point of budgeting, contract the talent—stars, writers, producers, directors, etc., and only then do they bring it to the studio for financing.

In that sense, the studio is much like a bank and the prodco like a property development company. All the costs of finding and evaluating scripts, securing material for the story, locating the actors, setting the budget, etc. are absorbed by the prodco. The costs of financing and distribution are absorbed by the studio and sometimes split with other entities—banks, other studios, other production companies, and so on.

But the result of all of this is an amazing number of conflicts that lead to delays, more conflicts, frustrations, bankruptcies, more delays and failed projects—and sometimes, brilliant films.

There was a time when actors, directors, producers, and writers all worked for the studio (kind of the way big agencies package their talent today—see WIK 10). The studio boss decided what he wanted to make and he put the contract employees to work. If another studio wanted a particular star, they had to negotiate his services from his home studio. The result of this stable of talent was similar to the Nabisco Company putting out cookies—movies rolled off the lot.

In the beginning, theaters were even owned by the studios. So if you wanted to see a Paramount movie, you could only see it in a Paramount Theater. The theater monopoly was quickly broken up—even though many of those same alignments exist today with studio ownership of network television. Disney movies are fairly exclusive to ABC and ABC Family, Fox to Fox, etc. Disney still owns a theater on Hollywood Boulevard called the El Capitan, which hosts the premier of most of its new movies.

In fact, it seems apparent that the majority of cost involved in marketing is the money the studio pays itself for commercial time in and on its own TV networks, magazines, newspapers, cell phones and internet companies—just another way to hide money from the government. After all, Murdoch owns Fox, MySpace, and half the newspapers and magazines on the planet. Sumner Redstone owns Viacom, which includes most big cable stations such as MTV, BET, VH1, and Comedy Central, as well as CBS, DreamWorks, Blockbuster, and Paramount. Time/Warner owns AOL and the other third of the media. And NBC owns Universal. So who else is getting all this marketing money?

As heads of studios decided to move on, or were fired, they formed production companies to make their own movies and sell them back to the studio for more money than they could make as employees. Eventually, studios lost their grip on talent. Actors, directors, writers and all began going to the highest bidder or the best project. And so on, and so on, until you have the current system of independent collaborators all trying to get on the same page long enough to get projects made. With such complicated machinery at work, the slightest clog can throw off an entire project.

For instance, I read on IMDB (the Internet Movie Database) that Halle Berry had been scheduled to star in a film, which was then put on hold until Halle had her baby. (That's power, by the way--perhaps a $100M project just waiting for her.) Now, Halle, of course, will be fine. But what about the young actor who scored the supporting role in the film? What about the new producer who mortgaged his house to buy the rights to the script two years ago and has been doing nothing but trying to secure Halle for this part for the last year and a half? What about the writer who... You get the point. Those lower folk are far more susceptible to problems caused by the delays and may have been in rehab by the time Halle came back.

In March, Halle had a baby girl, Nahla Ariela ...ahh. A lot of people have been waiting for you, little Nahla. Welcome to Hollywood.

A guy I met when I first came out here wrote a script about a superstar black major league baseball player who gets hit by a wild pitch and is knocked back into the old Negro leagues. It's a great story of humility, relating how this man learns to respect not only the game, but also the struggle that made his superstar status possible. In the process he meets his dad as a Negro league player—he'd never known him before he got knocked back in time.

Striking, right? Never made. Optioned twice for one year for $100,000 each time—once by Disney through the writer's fellowship, in which the writer participated, and once by Fox through the efforts of John Singleton. Neither Disney nor Singleton at Fox could get it made.

Finally, Will Smith bought the script outright for $250,000. My man got paid a total of $450,000 and never has had a single credit to his name. Why? Because the script is sitting in a drawer at Will's house somewhere while Will is busy making $20M zombie and superhero movies. Can't say that I blame Will, but this talented brother long ago spent that cash. He told me this story in 2002 and it was two years old then. The script got him a house in Venice Beach—which has no doubt doubled in value, but still, it's not the career he deserves.

Crap like that happens. And that's good crap. I wish someone would buy my script four times and put it in a drawer. No, I don't. That's not why I write. But the money would help.

My own experiences run to the level of absurd. One of my scripts eventually made it to a VP at Edmonds Filmed Entertainment named Tracy Kemble. Tracy had been a VP at HBO and, before that, was VP at Rush Entertainment with Russell Simmons and Stan Lathan. Tracy loved my script and said as soon as Tracey Edmonds (the once and immediately former Mrs. Eddie Murphy) gave her approval, she wanted to take it into HBO. Tracey Edmonds said fine.

Now, this is how I heard the story from my agent, Sandy. Sandy said that Tracy Kemble got into a horrible car accident in New York and was comatose for some months. By the time she came out of her situation, she was having a difficult time recuperating and had to resign her position at Edmonds.

That's a horrible situation for Tracy, whom I understand is fine now and living in New York. I can't be mad about what happened. It's just unfortunate all the way around. My project was her project and it died at Edmonds when she resigned her position. Why? Because a new exec will not continue to develop an old exec's projects. Why? Because, if the project succeeds, the old exec will get the credit. And if it fails, the new exec will get the blame. What about the writer? The who?

How many stories die in Hollywood because some producer, director, or agent got a divorce, went bankrupt, or got caught with a hooker on *Cheaters*? How many frustrated writers, actors, singers, dancers and directors gave up because of the difficulty of getting worthy projects off the ground, while watching *Dude, Where's My Car 4* hit theaters? It happens.

I actually fell asleep in the theater on *The Incredible Hulk, Spiderman 3, Ghost Rider* and *Fantastic Four: Rise of the Silver Surfer* (cool poster though, it's hanging above my head as I write this)—all $100M+ movies, all made off Marvel comics, all super-hyped and all...disappointing. They even bored my twelve-year-old daughter. Yet a studio exec would say, "Perhaps, but you went to see them, and we got paid, so it doesn't matter." Unfortunately, that's true.

Here's the reasoning behind this WIK. If you don't know that crap like this happens, you tend to take it personally or make a much bigger deal than you should. And depending on how you deal with this stuff happening, you could easily end up discouraged, angry, bitter, or saying the wrong thing at the wrong time.

My bitterness hit its zenith in early 2006. I'd been fully six months into a mild depression after firing Sandy and hearing from Peter that he was quitting to go work for Loyola Marymount.

The years I had worked to get an agent seemed so pointless and I found myself starting to have the kind of Hollywood writer's life that Eszterhas talked about in his book—okay, not as bad as Eszterhas, but not as good either. Very sadly, I did end up having marital problems and getting thrown out of my house by my amazingly good wife.

Hotel life didn't agree with me. All the better hotels seemed to stay booked in Burbank. I'd check into some joint at 1 a.m. alone and I'd leave by checkout the next morning, because I wasn't sure if I was going to stay there another night or find a better hotel room. But then I'd return the next night at 1 a.m., not having secured better accommodations. That just screams, "Screw up."

Just a few weeks earlier, we'd invested in a rental property that was sitting empty in Burbank, so rather than waste the hundred plus bucks a night on a hotel room—especially since the house was already losing a $150/day in mortgage costs, I took an airbed over there and set it up on the hardwood floor of one of the bedrooms.

The whole house was hardwood and empty—no stove, no fridge, no couch, no carpet, no nothing. I didn't intend to stay separated from my wife, but how long I would be wasn't clear to me either.

Did I mention there was no gas? There was electricity and running water—running *cold* water. I caulked the crevices in the floor to keep insects from coming up to get me in the night. I deserved to be gotten, karmically speaking, so I wasn't taking any chances. Even though the house had just been tented for termites and everything in it killed, there were still droppings in the corner of the kitchen. Why the hell am I telling you this? Oh....

Anyway, I was down and out in Burbank. I had sheets on the windows... you get the point. Here, in the middle of my Eszterhas experience, I get a call from Jeremy Kleiner.

Jeremy had just finished talking to Peter Heller and found out that Peter was no longer in the business, and wanted to know what was up with me. Being at the lowest point in my life and not feeling at all spiritual, or even particularly nice, I bemoaned to Jeremy that I was sick of the Hollywood bullshit and had simply lost all desire to write or do anything. Jeremy said I was extremely talented and I shouldn't give up. He said he didn't want to see me fall through the cracks and wanted to set up a meeting to have "dinner or drinks" with me as soon as possible. I took a deep breath and anticipated a fresh round of Hollywood bull.

Here it was six months after I'd lost Peter and fired Sandy. I hadn't written a thing. I was living on the floor of a nasty rental house because my wife had transferred all our money into a separate account, except for $7K I'd managed to swipe back via a found blank check.

I was living on the floor of an empty house with no heat in the beginning of February. Yes, it's Southern California, but remember it gets cold here at night (40 degrees)—especially in February. I was depressed. I was bitter. I was sick of Hollywood and I was having an Eszterhas moment (without the benefit of cocaine, tequila or Sharon Stone) and here was this former assistant to the Donners, this lucky little bastard who'd just wandered out of college a couple years before and landed a dream job with one of the gods of Hollywood, calling me up to have "dinner or drinks." It was surreal.

Peter told me Jeremy had gotten another dream job, over at Plan B—a company owned by two other Hollywood icons, Brad Pitt and Brad Grey—as an assistant to Brad Grey.

I was not in the mood for apples at the Four Seasons anymore. I told Jeremy I appreciated all he did to help me—sending my script to Peter and the subsequent experiences I'd had. I thanked him for caring, but said I really wasn't interested in "any more Hollywood bullshit."

He said he totally understood and appreciated my honesty. He'd had his share of bullshit too and wasn't interested in giving me any. *Good, now leave me alone.* But he insisted. I relented. Okay, one meeting. I owed him that. "When do you want to meet?"

And with that he said, "Hold on, let me check my calendar." *Is he kidding me? Check his calendar?* "I'll have to call you back, T.R.." *I can't believe the coconut balls on this guy—I'm gonna kick him in them when I see him.*

"Okay, call me back, Jeremy." If sarcasm could liquefy and drip from my lips, I'd need a bib.

"I will." And oddly enough, about twenty minutes later, I get a call... from Jason.

"Hi, T.R., this is Jason, Jeremy Kleiner's assistant." I wondered if it was the same Jason from Larry's office because they sounded alike. "Jeremy wanted me to call you to set up a meeting for drinks. How's 7 p.m. on Monday?"

Now I know Brad Grey is busy, but his assistant has an assistant? And he actually uses him to make his appointments? Only in Hollywood. I noted that he'd settled on drinks instead of dinner. Too bad. I could have used a free dinner at the time.

"Seven sounds fine, Jason." It was Wednesday. And, without my telling you, you know what happened on Monday...

Jason called to reschedule. "Some major investors are in town and Jeremy has to be there."

"Of course he does." So Jason reschedules me for one week out. For some reason, Hollywood meetings are always scheduled for the next week—never the next day. Maybe people think this makes them appear busier and, thus, more important. It's just more posturing.

I tried to get out of it. I knew I was unstable and I can't trust myself when I'm feeling unstable. Besides, what's the point of meeting Brad Grey's assistant anyway? "Next Monday? You know, Jason...I really don't see a need to do this. Jeremy's obviously very busy."

"No, he really wants to meet with you, but next Monday is the soonest."

And for some reason, it hit me to ask— probably because I was about to snap, "What's Jeremy do over there that he's so busy?"

"Well...uh...he's president of production."

I obviously had been bitten by something on the floor that night because I could swear that this guy just told me that the guy who was calling me was President of Production at Plan B—a company owned by one of the biggest producers and biggest actors in the world.

The hell he is! I thought I said, but I guess what came out was simply, "What?"

"He's president of production."

I found my senses. Peter had come through for me. He wasn't an asshole after all.

"Ok. In that case, next Monday's fine." Oh, my God did I get amped up. It all came rushing back to me—the pain of all those years was finally going to pay off. I couldn't believe it. My whole world was about to turn right side up. And boy would my wife be sorry she threw me out.

I started reviewing scripts I hadn't read in eight months. I started trying to figure out what I had that might work for Brad Pitt. "*ELIJAH!*" Yeah, that's right, I wanted him to play Elijah. And Angelina Jolie would make the perfect Jezebel with that Mediterranean look she's got. Oh yeah, baby. This is magic. God doesn't hate me after all. I don't have to become an alcoholic. Yes! Oprah and Will and Tony Robbins were all right. Follow that bliss, baby. Bliss!

Do I need to say what happened that Thursday? It involves my phone ringing and an assistant named Jason. I explained my gap theory earlier, right?

"Jeremy needs to reschedule to the seventh. He's got to go to Paris, blah... blah... blah..."

That's literally what I heard right before I channeled Eszterhas and heard myself say something I don't think I'd ever said to another individual in my life. "Well Jason, tell Jeremy I said, go f--k himself." Except I can't speak with dashes, so I pronounced the actual word.

"T.R., he really wants to meet, I'm very sorry."

"Tell Jeremy that I told him I didn't want anymore of this Hollywood bullshit and that I said to go f--k himself. And you go f--k yourself, too, Jason." And I hung up the phone in the middle of him stuttering.

I was in my mortgage office when I said that. People were staring at me in shock. But I felt a burst of energy like I'd never felt in my life. I was a man again—a grown-ass man. A stupid, grown-ass man. I had my Eszterhas moment without ever having to have even a tiny bit of his success. Maybe it was a Cleveland thing.

But my phone rang again. This time it was Jeremy himself—suddenly capable of using a phone—his cell phone—to call me. "T.R., look, it's unavoidable. I'm truly sorry..."

"Jeremy, I told you how I was feeling. This is the second reschedule and he's pushing me out three weeks. I can't take this, man. I'm serious. I'm so tired of this shit."

"T.R., I understand, it's nothing personal. I have no reason to jerk you around like this. I mean, think about it. I'm having this meeting for you.

There's no benefit in it for me. I'm doing it for you. I want to help you out."

Something about the way he said there was no benefit in it for him that insulted me even though I'd been the one out of order. "Jeremy, if there's no benefit in it for you, why are you wasting your time and mine?"

"T.R., let me reschedule. When I get back from Paris, we can sit down, ok? I'm going to have Jason call you back." I didn't respond, and Jeremy hung up. But Jason did call back. He left me a message because I didn't answer the phone. It said the seventh—three weeks out. I never responded.

On the morning of the seventh I got another voicemail. Jeremy would need to reschedule again. This time, I didn't bother calling back because I'd never had the appointment, as far as I was concerned. This time I text-messaged both of them. The text message said:

> *No need to reschedule. Never penciled you in. BTW, remember to go f--k yourselves. Peace, TRL.*

No dashes then, either. Childish? Yup. Stupid? Oh so very. Especially since the next year the 2007 Oscars had two Best Pictures nominated connected to Brad Pitt and, thus, to Plan B—*The Departed* (won best pic, actor and adapted screenplay, I think—ironically Nicholson was in that, too) and *Babel*. Both were great movies. I sat there watching and thinking *what if?*

But oddly enough, I also felt very encouraged about my writing talent. There was a sense of pride that the same folk who liked my stuff made those films. It was unfortunate I'd killed my relationship with them, but I felt encouraged anyway.

WIK crap happens and that sometimes it's uncontrollable and, even though some excuses sound crazy, it doesn't mean they aren't true.

WIK the nature of this business is uncertain and how to embrace that uncertainty and appreciate the process instead of bemoaning it.

Maybe if I'd known, I would have taken more time getting here and lowered my expectations a bit. At the very least, I wouldn't have said that to Jeremy and Jason.

In some way, I'd become what I told my writing group I wanted to become—again, though, without the success.

Here's the rest of that e-mail to my writing group after the meeting that prompted me to write this book. I didn't consciously try to become the writer I describe in this e-mail, but it amazes me that I became him anyway.

>*I was hugely pissed off at Larry. So I rewrote the scene to fit the persona of the writer I want to be someday. Everything stays the same up to the point where we get in the office:*
>
>*Larry comes on the phone and asks, "Whatcha got?" Then this is how it goes...*
>
>*"Larry, I've got this great story. It's about a movie producer who makes three okay movies then gets this big head. He thinks he's a hot shot around town..."*
>
>*"Wait, wait... I thought this was about the last white man living in a black neighborhood or something? With Nicholson, no?"*
>
>*"No. I don't want to pitch that one anymore. This one's much better. You'll love it. The guy's a real ass-- canceling meetings on people at the last minute and what not. Goin' round like he's Bruckheimer.... Then one day he calls in this new writer who drives all the way across town to meet him. But the catch is, he's canceled this guy twice already, right?"*
>
>*"Okay, I follow, but this sounds like something I've seen before."*
>
>*"No, hold up... The writer shows up. And this son of a bitch isn't even there. He's going to take the meeting over the phone. But what's worse, when he gets online, the guy is rushing the writer so he's all uncomfortable, you know?"*
>
>*"Yeah, I like it. The producer's time is money."*
>
>*"Right. And the writer's time is dog piss."*
>
>*"Writers are overrated."*
>
>*"Exactly. And it's got a great title."*

"What genre is it?"

"It's a thriller. Or maybe just a dark comedy."

"Gimme the title!"

"It's called, 'F--k You and The Horse You Rode In On.' And get this ending..."

At that point, I pick up the handset and slam it down in the cradle. Then I smile at the stunned Gil and say, "You think you guys might want to buy it?"

As I exit Gil's office, I order Jason to validate my parking stub, but I stand three feet away from him and make him come get it.

On the way out, the receptionist asks, "How'd it go?"

I tell her it was great, but I don't think he liked it because it had a female lead, and, "Your boss doesn't think women can open movies."

I became that writer without even an inkling of success. I guess if I want to be a self-absorbed jerk, nothing stops me. I'm just not sure it's good for anything. Reminds me of a joke:

On reaching his plane seat, a man is surprised to see a parrot strapped in the seat next to him. The man asks the stewardess for a cup of coffee and the parrot squawks, "And get me a whisky, bitch."

The flustered stewardess brings back a whisky for the parrot but forgets the man's coffee.

As the man nicely points out the omission to the stewardess, the parrot downs his drink and squawks, "Another whisky, hag."

Visibly shaken, the stewardess brings the parrot's whisky, but still no coffee.

The man decides to try the parrot's approach. He says, "I've asked twice for a cup of coffee, wench. Get it now!"

Suddenly, two burly stewards grab both the man and the parrot and throw them out the emergency exit.

Plunging to the ground the parrot turns to the man and says, "For someone who can't fly, you sure are a lippy bastard."

That's one reason why I can't talk like Eszterhas. I don't have my wings. I got caught at a bad time and I let my emotions get the best of me. I wish I knew then what I know now. But I guess Hollywood had me feeling a little like the subject in this one:

A woman was shaking out a rug on the balcony of her seventeenth floor condo when a gust of wind blew her over the railing.

As she passed the fourteenth floor, a man caught her in his arms. While she looked at him in disbelieving gratitude, he asked, "Do you suck?"

"No!" she shrieked, aghast. So, he dropped her.

As she passed the twelfth floor, another man reached out and caught her. "Fancy a screw?" he asked.

"Of course not!" she exclaimed before she could stop herself. He dropped her too.

The poor woman prayed to God for one more chance. A man on the eighth floor was the third person to catch her. "I suck! I screw!" she screamed in panic.

"Slut!" he said, and dropped her.

I guess I just didn't have what they were looking for. When I don't have what they're looking for, I can't please them anyway, so the best idea is to be authentically me. What's great about being a creative artist is that, even if no one reads my stuff but me, I'll still find happiness writing it.

If you start to feel that way too, maybe one day they'll come around to where you are. But if not, you know what to do with them and the horses they rode in on. Next time, read a book instead of going to see *Daddy Day Care 5*, or paying to download the latest song that sounds like the twenty others before it.

Even though it may be frustrating to be overlooked for whatever reason, remember...

Be Careful Not to Put New Wine in Old Wineskins

This warning from the Bible has to do with what happens in the old method of winemaking. When wine was preserved in skins rather than barrels, as it is today, the skin would expand as the wine fermented and gasses built up. An old wineskin was one that had been used to make wine and therefore was stretched to its limit.

If new wine was placed in the old wineskin, the old wineskin would burst when the new wine fermented and all the wine, and therefore time and labor taken to produce it, would be lost.

Even though situations are often similar and the point of this book is to alert you to things you should know about Hollywood, there is a persistent dichotomy that must be recognized, too.

Simply put, each individual, agent, producer, lawyer, manager, etc., has a unique relationship with you. They come with their baggage and you come with your baggage; but just because the last guy lied to you whenever he opened his mouth, doesn't mean this new guy will too.

The fine line I walk as I write these pages is between advice intended to protect you from emotional and mental damage, and bellyaching or fear-mongering that discourages you from trying. Although I titled this "What I Wish I Knew Before I Moved To Hollywood," it's inevitable that, for some people who read this book, the stories will be so discouraging that they'll abandon the idea of following their dreams. That's not my goal.

My goal is to help you see the path more clearly and to avoid obstacles. For me, many of the obstacles were mental attitudes I developed after having my heart broken by one of the realities (WIKs) I described in this book. It's taken me two-and-a-half years to get back on the path. One of the main reasons is because I kept putting new wine in old wineskins.

Whether your heart has been broken by lovers or by people screwing around with your dreams, it's easy to develop defense systems that unfairly judge anyone who comes near your heart. Sometimes those sentries signal danger to and turn away the very ones we wish to draw into our lives.

My reaction to Jeremy Kleiner canceling his meeting with me was due to my displaced anger over my postponed and cancelled meetings with Larry Kennar. I put Jeremy's new wine in the old wineskin I'd stretched out dealing with Larry. Therefore, I mistakenly gave to Jeremy the "screw yourself" I wanted to give to Larry.

Whether you transfer anger you have at your spouse to your children, or shift the anger you feel at your boss to your spouse, or the anger at your old agent gets displaced onto your new agent, it's still wrong.

On top of that, it's very hard to find that balance that allows you to know when someone is blowing smoke up your dress versus when they are really interested in advancing your career. Ultimately you can't really know until the check is cashed and clears the bank. So on some level you have to be willing to trust in order to make it in Hollywood, but don't trust completely. The fact remains that this business is flaky at best and the folk in it are flakier.

But to make sure you don't miss out on any good thing unnecessarily, give each individual his or her own new wineskin and let them stretch it out with their own gasses.

Hollywood Will Test Your Personal Relationships Severely

L et me put it this way: there aren't very many happily married couples in Hollywood. Some might argue there aren't very many happily married couples anywhere, but I believe wedded bliss is rarer in Hollywood. Even couples who appear happy and strong often turn out to be together only for convenience, or until their new movie premiers or album drops.

This isn't just true of married couples; it's true of relationships at any level. Hollywood has a way of testing the bonds of all types of relationships.

I think it's important to make a clear distinction at this point. There is the decision to come to Hollywood to pursue a dream... and there is being in Hollywood. The decision to come begins with desire and belief as I outlined in the chapter, "What Was I Thinking?"

Deciding to pursue a dream, in itself, has a powerful effect on relationships. Once you're in Hollywood, however, the town itself has other effects.

When I sent out the first draft of this book to my writing group to read and evaluate, a number of them were shocked to find out I had separated from my wife, Lisa, for a while. Luckily, I came to my senses, and she took me back in, and we've reaffirmed our love and commitment. But a number of readers pointed out that the effect Hollywood has on relationships is something that deserves a deeper look.

My wife and I had had a great many discussions before deciding to sell our stuff and move here. The idea of moving so far away from family seemed both crazy and exciting. California is undeniably beautiful when you visit; and regardless of where you come from, the Mediterranean climate is a huge plus, unless you prefer cold, rain and snow.

It wasn't a hard sell. We debated and decided we'd give it a shot. We figured we had enough money to live on for two years, and we possessed what I believed was a film deal in the hand and one in the bush.

Obviously, things didn't turn out as planned. There is a resentment that can set in when one partner gives up comforts to help another pursue a dream and that dream doesn't come to pass as expected. But it's an almost equal resentment that can build up if one partner is unwilling to give up comforts to help the other pursue a dream. Check out this e-mail from a member of my writing group:

> *Part of my trepidation in moving my family out here is the fear that I would not live up to everything I said I was going to do. Well I guess the fact that I'm here now says that I didn't let those worries deter me. But here I am, jobless and broke with my family in pretty dire straits. I look at the caller ID now before I answer the phone to dodge bill collectors. It is affecting my marriage to the point that my husband and I are barely speaking. Part of what makes him happy is providing for his family. He feels he has regressed to when he first started working—to the time when we were living check to check trying to save and buy a house. He worked so hard and now he has nothing to show for it. On top of that he feels betrayed by me for not holding up my end of the bargain, which was to find a job and help him out*

now that we were paying for our old mortgage [since our home back east hasn't sold] and paying rent here that is double our old mortgage. I got a job temping but that didn't last. And all because I came here so focused on what I wanted—to get staffed on a TV show. When the writers strike happened, I dropped into depression. Needless to say things are not great between us.

Her story isn't uncommon. A key factor in any relationship is remembering that nothing is guaranteed in pursuing this dream. As I pointed out earlier, pursuing this dream is a roll of the dice even for a remarkable artist. Talent doesn't guarantee success. The resentment my colleague's husband feels is a mourning of things lost in the bet they made. Had she succeeded, he would have happily taken the winnings.

The second problem mentioned in this e-mail is one we experienced as well. We began to run out of money almost two years into living here. Lisa had been a stay-at-home mom before we left Chicago. Between our properties and my job, she was used to a comfortable life.

Around the time we started running out of money I was close to securing an agent. I was completely focused on writing and learning the movie business.

Meanwhile, back in Chicago, the tenants we had living in our last remaining rental house suddenly moved out and left the house in shambles. We located contractors long distance to prepare the house to be sold. We had two contractors run off with our deposits. Finally we got the work done. It cost us thousands of dollars. We had to put the cost on our credit cards— maxing some of them out in the process.

During the time the rental house was being worked on it was vacant and generating no income, so we were unable to pay the mortgage there in addition to our bills here. So the bank, which financed the house, accelerated the mortgage and demanded the full loan be paid or it would go into foreclosure. We owed $65,000 and neither of us had worked for almost two years so refinancing it was impossible. By the time the work on the house was done, the foreclosure had begun.

We listed it with a real estate broker in Chicago and before the broker could go by to take pictures, the house had been broken into and vandalized.

It seemed as if one bad thing after another happened. Lisa was in a near panic. She felt obligated to get a job. And she felt betrayed, too. I felt angry that she was sweating me about getting a job when I was so close to getting the agent I just knew would be the answer to our problems. There was significant tension. I felt she was losing faith in me. She felt I was shirking my responsibilities. I felt I'd worked long enough and hard enough in Chicago that I deserved the time to follow my dreams. She felt I'd had two years and now I could follow them while working.

Looking back on it, perhaps I was shirking responsibility, but I honestly believed the agent would lead to the work, so in my own way, I was looking for a job, too—just not in the traditional way.

Like my colleague in the e-mail above, this wasn't what I'd promised Lisa when we moved, but I was so close I could taste it. Like a poker player with only a few chips left, I went all-in and hoped for the best. Instead I busted out.

The buyers who eventually came to buy the Chicago rental property failed to get financing. The foreclosure was looming and, if it foreclosed, we would lose $75,000 in equity. My attorney in Chicago told me the only way to stop the foreclosure, and save that desperately needed $75,000, was to declare bankruptcy.

Lisa took a job she hated. Every day became a complaint session that led to a fight. And every day, despite my focus on writing, she looked for work for me, too. She eventually made a contact that led to me reluctantly taking a position at a mortgage company in Burbank. Once I did, she was able to quit the job she hated and start selling real estate.

We were back to making decent money, but not enough to save the rental house and its equity—the foreclosure was imminent. So we filed bankruptcy. I had indeed followed my bliss to bankruptcy.

Proudly though, we made it through that. In many ways, it was nice getting a fresh start—even though our credit was ruined. At least we still had each other. And by the time of the bankruptcy, I had an agent, too. Things weren't so bad. We made it through that struggle fairly easily. Two years later, though, it was another story.

I don't know that this tension is any different regardless of what dreams you choose to pursue. But it's something to consider before moving across the country and away from support systems.

Lisa had given up a 2,000 square foot house for a 1,000 square foot apartment. Though she admits now that the experiences we've had living in L.A. were worth it, at the time she was less positive. She was focused on getting back to the things we had had in Chicago. I wasn't.

Although just making it day-to-day in Hollywood is staggeringly difficult for many people, it wasn't so much the moving here, or the decision to follow a dream that caused Lisa and me to eventually separate. What hurt our marriage most was more a direct result of the rejection I faced once I got here.

If you're not used to rejection, suddenly encountering it in massive quantities can be devastating to your ego and open you up to any number of potential threats to your relationships—depression among them.

By the time I'd lived through the stories I've told in this book and fired Sandy, I wasn't sure which way was up anymore. I'd stopped writing everything but journal entries because I didn't see the point in it. I began to regret the choices I'd made and that self-condemnation took me deeper into the hole. Lisa watched me go from being a brilliant (her words, not mine) writer, full of enthusiasm, hope and talent, to being a jaded, depressed mortgage broker.

But worse than that, I experienced what I felt was the death of my dreams. Suddenly my life became mediocre—plain... unflavored... unscented... uncolored. In reality, it wasn't, but it felt that way compared to the Technicolor world I'd imagined awaited me in Hollywood.

All those hope-filled meetings at studios had become apples at the Four Seasons. My experience with my agent and manager had been nearly the opposite of what I expected. Firing Sandy produced only a temporary euphoria that quickly vanished when I realized my phone was no longer ringing with news of studios and producers who wanted to meet me.

My mind began to wander. While many of my colleagues in the mortgage business were earning between $50,000-$100,000 per month during the California real estate boom and couldn't get enough of the three times a week paydays, I found myself doing one or two lucrative deals, then not working for 3-6 months at a time. I kept the same car I came here with. I lived in the same apartment.

At the weekly softball game, my colleagues bragged about their new million dollar homes and showed off their new cars. I couldn't care less. I wasn't working much. I wasn't writing—except a ton of grievances against Hollywood in my journal. I had a lot of free time on my hands. I played a lot of tennis. I didn't realize it at the time, and I doubt people would say they could tell, but I'd sunk into depression.

In my mind, I'd already made a lot of money before and it failed to make me happy. My coming to Hollywood was about a dream, a purpose, and that dream seemed out of reach now because Hollywood was nothing like I'd expected it to be. It almost seemed as if my dream had been misguided from the beginning. Although no one at my company would have agreed with me, making money just wasn't the answer. But neither was the drama I ended up creating in my life because of the depression.

Not only was I not aware that I was experiencing depression, neither was Lisa. I unconsciously began to look for ways to spice up my life again. It would take over a year of therapy to finally understand that what I really needed to do was keep writing and learn not to personalize the rejection I'd experienced in my writing because it's just part of the game.

Knowing to expect rejections and not to take them personally or as a sign that you have no talent, as I wrote earlier, goes a long way towards helping to keep emotions in check and encourages partners to help each other through those rejections.

If we had it to do again, we would still come to Hollywood, but we would do it differently—aware of the pitfalls I've shared in this book. Most times it was the shock of learning the WIK moreso than the WIK itself that really hurt.

One final note about relationships being tested in Hollywood: In case you didn't know, Hollywood is full of distractions. By that I mean some of the best looking people in the world—many of them extremely friendly, intelligent, open, supportive, creative, driven, alone, horny and single; every type of drug, every type of lifestyle, and every type of entertainment. When things aren't right in one part of your life, it's often too easy to find a temporary fix in a bad place. But if you value your relationships, guard your heart, focus your mind and keep at your craft. What looks like an answer under the temporary stresses of depression, personal disagreements, disappointments, rejections and other pains will look very different in time.

It Could Well Be That What Inspires Your Creativity Most is Native to Your Hometown, Not Hollywood

P eople wonder why rappers who've succeeded in becoming big stars still hang out and often do the same things they did before they made it big. T.I. gets caught with machine guns with silencers on them, while he's already on probation? Stupid! Or Tupac and Biggy—the original bad boys.

I'm convinced that the concept of "keeping it real" is most related to the inspiration for their particular art. These guys are artists. But the inspiration for their art is shattered as soon as they become stars. It's very difficult to write about injustice and dirty cops when those cops are guarding your mansion and keeping your child safe at school.

So many times, a particular artistic expression is forged in a particular fire. As I wrote in the introduction, this very book would be impossible to write if I were already on the other side. If my agent and manager and I were lunching together at Hamburger Hamlet in Beverly Hills, and discussing my next million-dollar script, I wouldn't feel free to call them jerks... I wouldn't even want to. I wouldn't be thinking about the crap I've gone through in this town—let alone thinking about how to warn or educate others.

As I mentioned before, too, if you did your best writing—your best art— while it was raining or snowing outside, moving to L.A. may well kill your best art simply because it never snows, and it almost never rains.

I find it interesting that Oprah never relocated to L.A. She's from Mississippi, and she's black, so I know she's got to hate the cold of Chicago. She may have a home in Santa Barbara, but she lives in Chicago. I believe it's because she feels more authentically herself there. It's obviously paid off for her.

I wrote some of my best scripts while trapped in my downtown Chicago office looking out two giant windows to the John Hancock and Bloomingdale's Towers on Michigan Avenue. The sound of constant traffic two stories beneath me, the wind in the treetops, the rain and snow against the glass, and the lights of the city at night were inspirational. My drive home down the Dan Ryan, past the Robert Taylor projects, would bring me into contact with characters, scenes, and ideas.

I knew that if I moved I'd miss some of that. My next office was in my bedroom looking straight out on the Verdugo Mountains in Burbank. Palm trees and million-dollar hillside homes dotted the vista. I still had traffic noise two stories below me, but it was definitely different—especially the cast of characters surrounding me. A trip to the ghettos of L.A. was more like visiting a middle-class neighborhood in Chicago. There are no Starbucks in the ghettos in Chicago.

I think rappers were some of the first to figure this out. There are regional rap labels that seem to take turns having national hits now. Groups from Atlanta, St. Louis, and New Orleans each bring their own unique flavor the same way that groups from L.A. and New York did in the '80s and '90s. These artists stay in their respective areas and continue to produce songs popular with their audiences. When a song catches on nationally, it's a bonus, but it doesn't mean the artist is moving to Hollywood.

Staying in their hometowns may limit some national sales, but it helps insure the artist's product stays true to its roots. More importantly, it helps insure the artists stay true to their roots. And since Hollywood is about marketing, it even helps Hollywood sell those artists around the world.

It may well be that writers, producers, dancers and actors could see their careers bloom stronger by staying where they are planted. This isn't always the case, but it's something to consider if your art is influenced by your environment.

When you're in Hollywood, apart from a set on the Universal lot, the closest you come to the old, congested, big city feel of the east coast or Midwest towns like Chicago, New York, Detroit or Philly is San Francisco—five hours north. The closest you come to a cornfield is Nebraska and the closest you come to the woods, snow or a real lake is Big Bear—three hours east, in the mountains.

So consider what inspires your artistic expression. Before you move to Hollywood, make sure your muse won't be left behind in Downers Grove.

Don't Tell the President of Any Production Company to Go F- - k Himself or Send it to Him in a Text Message

I did discuss this, right? Well, it bears repeating. However, it's also true that...

Folks Here Change Positions Like Musical Chairs

Although he may be the president of production this month, no telling what he'll be next month.

Longevity isn't very common here. With many people on the way up and down, not many stay fixed anywhere for long. That's why it's so important to keep doing your art. Even if you do screw up, just stick around, and there'll be a fresh new group of newbies to practice your pitching on next year.

On that same note, use this reality as a caution to help you be careful not to say to anyone the kind of thing I said, no matter how furious or frustrated you become. Because execs change positions so much, it's not unusual to find the exec you cussed out at Disney suddenly in charge of your project at Sony.

Part III:
Alternative Realities

"It takes a person who is wide awake to make his dreams come true."
—Roger Ward

"My theory is that, if you look confident, you can pull off anything—even if you have no idea what you're doing."
—Jessica Alba

"There is a difference between knowing the path and walking the path."
—Morpheus

What They Know

I n the first draft of this book I used only my own experiences. One of my readers suggested that the experiences of others might add to the book's usefulness. Well, I knew already that many had experienced the frustrations I'd gone through, including that reader. I didn't really feel it was necessary to gather all the horror stories about Hollywood that I could find—although I might do that in a web site. Like I said earlier, I'm not trying to discourage you, just help prepare you. Besides, I knew so many stories already and they tend to all be variations on the themes I've already covered.

But what did make sense to me was the idea of including in this book some advice from folk who had made it in one way or another—people who had booked big movie roles, signed big record contracts, become TV stars, wrote successful movies or TV shows, won awards and gained fame—in other words, people who had lived in front of the Hollywood sign. What do they wish they knew? What would they have done differently if they could? What advice could they give someone looking to start in this business that could be helpful?

I didn't want it to be fluff, though. I didn't want it to be advice from people who'd never really struggled—stars who'd lucked up when they first came to Hollywood and booked their first audition, sailed to the top as if predestined and bought their mansion the year after they arrived. No. I wanted people who'd taken some time to make it, or made it fast and busted, and then had to figure a way to make it again.

But then I thought about the book. I've decided to speak my mind in this book in a way that might end up backfiring on me. I'm at a point in my career, though, where I don't care. I don't want to hurt people either inside or outside the industry, but I do want to speak the truth and I don't want to sugarcoat it so that others end up following their bliss blindly to the same bankruptcy I'd found.

I don't care about my Hollywood career being hurt by this book. But these actors, writers, editors, makeup artists, producers, comedians, TV, movie and music stars are still in this business. And some are at places of great vulnerability in their careers. On more than one occasion, during an interview, the artists would stop, pause, say they didn't want to be quoted on something, and pause again before couching their answer in the most inoffensive language possible. I could almost hear them asking themselves, "Who might read this book? Do I really want to say that?"

I had to reassure them that I wouldn't quote them in any way that would put them in a negative light. That presents a dilemma for me—a major dilemma. Do I quote them by name, gaining the credibility and marketability that would carry, and leave out the stuff that might harm them—thereby missing some of the best advice they offered? Do I phrase what they said in ways that are saccharine sweet and possibly lose the edginess? Ugh. I hate these decisions.

OR... do I just leave out their names altogether risking the inevitable suspicions of my more critical readers and losing the oomph some of their names carry?

I decided to go with the latter—to describe a bit of what they've done, not specifically enough for anyone to guess who they are, but enough to let you know they know what they're talking about. Then I can say everything they told me without fear of bringing any harm on their careers or repercussions from my interviewees for my failure to properly judge which quotes were harmful and which not. I'm actually very good at thinking some things are completely inert when, in fact, they are quite volatile—just ask my wife.

In my later interviews, I simply told them I would not use their names so that they spoke even more honestly and openly from the beginning.

The final reason for including these outside views is simple. I don't have experience as a makeup artist, a TV comedy writer, a record producer, a network executive or a Grammy nominated singer. There are many jobs here about which I have no knowledge except what I can gain from someone else. Maybe you're interested in one of these positions? I may not be able to scratch every Hollywood itch, but in getting info from other insiders, I may be able to shed some light on what to expect in those careers as well.

That said, my roster of interviewees has been collected from various relationships I have in Hollywood. Among them:

- The head makeup artist for a huge Fox television series.
- Two gold-selling pop and soul singers, one a Grammy nominated singer/songwriter.
- A well-known comedian with a ton of television and standup writing credits for some of the biggest comedians in the country.
- A young actor who got his first movie role starring opposite Denzel Washington, and later won a best actor award for his work in live theater.
- Another young actor whose first big role was opposite an Oscar-nominated actor.
- An actor/writer/producer who booked a number of small roles on TV before writing his first film, which he then sold to HBO.
- A 30-year acting veteran of movies and TV and now the lead actor of one of the most successful award-winning dramatic television shows on the air.
- A former actor, turned studio executive, turned singer, who's toured the world and performed at Carnegie Hall.
- A multi-platinum music producer of a Who's Who of hip-hop artists.
- A network TV executive with numerous projects in development at NBC.

If I've done my job right, you won't be sure who any of these people are, but you should be confident they have some advice that might help make your path a little smoother—or at least warn you of where some of the potholes are.

Behind The Scenes—Staffers:

Make Up Artist

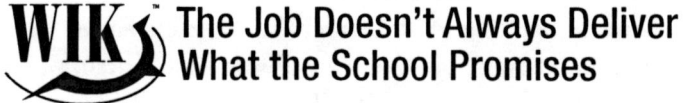 **The Job Doesn't Always Deliver What the School Promises**

Let's start with my makeup artist client/friend. I sought her advice quite innocently on behalf of a young man who works at the boxing gym I go to. He'd recently graduated make-up school and was looking for an internship for himself and his girlfriend, who was still attending the school. I thought my friend might be able to help them. I e-mailed her for her advice and received a startling reply that fits perfectly in this book. Rather than condensing it, I'll just paste it whole:

> *Hi T.R., Oh how difficult this situation can be for a young makeup person these days. Unfortunately there is no intern program in our union. The jobs in this field are few and far between. I can't imagine going into this business at this time. (THE MAKEUP SCHOOLS ARE GETTING RICH) I can only say that, HONESTLY, it will take them at least 10 years before they make a living at this. I would suggest that he tries a job at a makeup counter or if he does FX makeup possibly working in a lab. I can't bring any non-union people onto the studio lots. It really is a shame, because a good internship would be beneficial to our young artists. Just tell them that they have to hang in there & catch a break. Between us, the schools SELL these kids a bill of goods. Out of every 50 students maybe one makes it. I*

wish I could be more helpful and upbeat but I am being really honest. I'm sorry I couldn't help but on the positive side, maybe he's the one who makes it!   Take care.

You can't get any more real than that. And, in fact, she is the one who prompted me to include the advice of the pros in this anonymous way. When I thanked her for her response, I asked her for permission to quote her in this book. She didn't want that. I figured as much when she wrote "between us." So it's anonymous. But it's out there for your benefit.

It's easy to believe that getting work behind the scenes is easier than getting work in front of the camera, but that's not always so. Granted, when you watch the credits roll at the end of a film, it's quite obvious that many more people worked on the film than appeared in it, but that doesn't mean it's easier to get one of those jobs, most of which can be very hard to come by.

When I first came to Hollywood, I moved into an apartment in Burbank. After 9/11, the building managers decided to have a get-together so that neighbors in the building could meet each other and just talk about things. I met people who were accountants for studios, animators, video game designers, computer techs at studios, actors, agents, parents of child actors, and holders of assorted other peripheral jobs in the industry.

One animator I met worked at Disney Animation. It sounded like one of the coolest jobs I could imagine. I asked him if I'd seen any of his work. He said, "Well, I worked on *Tarzan*." Wow. I asked him what he animated. I can't remember the exact thing he said, but it was some *minutiae* related to the way that one group of the animals moved during the musical sequences. "I worked on that for three years," he said glumly, "and they only used ten seconds of what I'd done."

I didn't think I'd heard him right. Three years? I can only imagine him as a kid growing up, dreaming of working for Disney Animation. He got the dream, but it wasn't what he expected it to be at all. He certainly didn't seem happy. But then again, at least Disney used some of what he'd done. I'm sure that's not true for all animators.

Perhaps he'll do more on the next movie. But it's interesting to note that, at the time of our conversation in 2001, *Tarzan* had been out for two years. He'd worked on it for three years before that. My daughter was six, so I'd seen every Disney movie since 1995. He didn't mention having worked on any others.

Jobs don't always deliver on what the schools promise. Of course that's true of more places than Hollywood, but it is certainly true here, too.

Network TV Executive

When your ex is one of Eddie Murphy's former writing and production partners, you get to meet a lot of people and see a lot of things in L.A. This TV exec didn't move to L.A. though; she was born here.

"I find it interesting that people move here to be in this business. I never really thought about it. To me, this is just working downtown," she told me in the NBC commissary next door to where *The Tonight Show with Jay Leno* films. "But I guess my ex moved here to write, so I understand the drive that an artist can have and what that's like."

WIK The Real TV World is Nothing Like on TV

"I grew up watching movies and thinking the whole world inside the TV was magical. Everything seemed so perfect and anything could happen. It's quite different working here day to day and seeing how they do it. I never knew it would look like this," she said waving her hand around at the studio lot outside the window.

It was striking having this conversation in this particular place. As we walked to the commissary, I'd told her that the idea behind the book was the life behind the Hollywood sign. While walking we passed within a few hundred feet of the back of Mt. Hollywood and past trucks, dollies, scaffolds, security gates; through giant sound stages, around tour groups, past painters, carpenters, and other busy construction workers. From where we sat in the commissary, it seemed like the lunchroom of any other large company.

WIK To Blend into This Industry, You Must Sacrifice

Being an exec at a TV studio is not exactly the creative track, even though there's plenty of opportunity to be involved in creating new shows. It's more a corporate track with beginnings that sound like something fresh off *The Apprentice*.

"I got a call the other day from a young lady [I know personally] who'd just gotten placed as an intern in the creative development department. She was complaining because all she was doing was moving boxes all day long. She didn't seem to realize that she was in one of the best departments to intern and she's going to have to be aggressive if she wants someone to take her under their wing. It's up to her to grab someone by the arm and ask, 'Will you teach me how to do what you do?' If they say 'no,' then grab someone else. These people here are busy; they don't have time to spoon-feed you. I wanted to shake her and tell her there are hundreds of young hungry college grads begging to have the opportunity you have. Wake up!

"This is a very competitive business. You nearly have to sell your soul. You really have to give up a lot of yourself to blend in here. And this is still not as bad as over at William Morris or CAA [Creative Artists Agency]. I hear over there they tell them right off the bat, 'You've got seven months. If you're not working with an agent or we're not talking to you about coming on board, you'd better know where you're going, because you won't be working here.' And off they go stabbing each other in the backs for seven dollars an hour.

"You get these Ivy League grads every so often with a sense of entitlement. They have this attitude like they've already earned their position. It's funny. They're like, 'I went to Brown.' And I'm like, 'Oh, really? Well go get coffee for the whole office, then toast a bagel for me.'" She laughs. "I had to do it, you will too. We all go through the same fire.

"Back when I'd gotten my first promotion, the girl who replaced me called constantly asking me how to do this or how to do that. I finally had to tell her, 'Figure it out like I did. I'm busy.'

"It takes at least five years to start to gain back some of what you give up to get going in this industry—a lot of time for very little pay."

 ## Small Things Can Lead to Big Things

"I got this job through temping. I didn't want to do NBC that day. But the guy who ran the service said he really needed someone and I really needed the money. I was recently separated from my ex and things were crazy. I ended up working really well with the exec. When I came, she was trying to develop this show for Bravo. She was working until 9pm every night. I was like, 'I have to go home.' My ex was downstairs flashing the lights of the car, but she wouldn't let me leave. I just had to get up and go. And the next day it would be the same thing.

"But she liked me and asked me to come with her when she took her new position. I was the only one who could stand to work with her.

"It takes a while, but interns work their way up the ladder to assistants, to staff to managers to executives. Along the way you learn the rules of the corporate game, who the power players are and how to position and align yourself strategically for your best chance at success.

"My ex could never do that. He wrote with Eddie and didn't know anything about the regular working world. He wanted to be a writer and that was it. I didn't get it. There's nothing wrong with being a writer, but can't you get a job in the meantime?"

WIK This Work is a Strain and Drain on Families

"I work my job here, but now I have three projects in development as well. You meet people along the way and you start putting things together. If I hadn't had the office assistant job, I wouldn't have the chance to have these projects in development now.

"When Eddie decided he didn't want to have his production company anymore, that was it. My ex didn't know what to do. He got dropped off in the middle of Bakersfield" (meaning left high and dry). "He still lives in the world where everything could change at the very next moment. And it could. But it's hard to build a life on 'could.'

"That's how it is for writers. They get used to the writing life and they don't fit well back in the workplace or the job world. He can't imagine working a regular job. That was very hard to deal with."

WIK All You Have to Do to Become a Celebrity is Release a Sex Tape

"As far as things I wish I knew before I got into this business...how about the fact that all you have to do to be a celebrity these days is release a sex tape." We laugh. "That would have been a much easier road."

WIK 23 Pay Attention to the Trends in Your Industry

"I think it would have helped if I'd paid closer attention to the trends in the industry. I didn't realize things were moving the way that they did in terms of digital distribution. It seems I looked up one day and it suddenly went from suits to kids. Social networking is how we talk to each other now. It works well for viral [marketing] stuff, but I wish I'd seen it coming and been better prepared."

The next couple of guys have achieved success in multiple career fields in Hollywood. It stands to reason that they have lots of advice.

Hyphenates—Multi-talented artists:

Hyphenate #1 — Actor-Writer-Singer

This artist came to Hollywood back in the '80s after a decent career on the live stage in New York. He initially booked a number of roles on television, but soon saw those opportunities dwindle.

I've always found it interesting to know how actors make their living while trying to break into acting. A writer can write anytime—late at night, after work, early in the morning. But acting is a very sporadic job that often requires you to drive all over town on days you have auditions, and may leave you with absolutely nothing to do on days you don't. It's imperative that an actor either has a job that allows him this freedom or that he work at night. That's why so many actors are waiters.

This particular actor worked for a catering company. A number of actors I interviewed did the same thing. Catering companies work on a per day basis—they call you up and check if you're available a day or so in advance and, if you work it right, it's possible to bring home upwards of $500/week.

After arriving in Hollywood and seeing his opportunities start to dry up, this actor began helping out any way he could on the set of a sitcom on which he'd had a bit part. When he'd previously lived in New York, he'd worked on stage with one of the lead actresses on the sitcom. Because of his relationship with her and his affable nature, he endeared himself to some of the production staff and was offered a chance to work with one of the producers who had a deal with NBC.

WIK ᴊ Start as Young as You Can and Make as Many Friends as Possible— Especially Before They Make It in the Biz

According to this actor, one of the realities of Hollywood is that relationships you make on your way up often turn into money at a later date. This might sound contrary to WIK #7 but it's not because, as this actor put it, there are two ways that relationships with people in Hollywood will help you:

1. "If you're young and the other person is older, they will often help you because you remind them of themselves when they were younger."
2. "If you knew them before they made it they will often not only help you, but also put you on their team for the long haul." (e.g., Nicholson and Mort.)

"However, if you are older, successful people are often suspicious of you because they wonder why you haven't 'gotten yours' and they assume that something must be wrong with you because you haven't broken through yet." In reality, you may have just started late, but Hollywood is a young person's town. Usually people start here very early. This actor's advice is "the earlier, the better."

Once at NBC, he found himself shuffling off to meeting after meeting giving notes to writers and making sure producers and actors had what they needed. When he saw his opportunity, he helped an up-and-coming comedian develop a sitcom that later got picked up by the network. To his surprise though, the comedian didn't hire him to write on the show. So following the advice he gave about helping people before they get big in the business won't always bear fruit. Sometimes they just use you and pretend they did it all by themselves.

Unfortunately what should have worked in his favor—his likeable nature—turned out to draw the envy of his superiors. "They were jealous because the actors liked me—liked working with me. When I wasn't around, they'd ask for me. When that happened, the guys above me started making things very hard for me."

Although the comedian didn't think much of him, someone who did was the young lady he was dating, who happened to be best friends with a music promoter. "Come to think of it, a lot of gigs came from the ladies I was, quite frankly, trying to have sex with at the time," he said. Perhaps another piece of advice is that intimate relationships can have many different benefits.

Very near the time he was ready to quit NBC, he received a call asking him to sing backup for a famous Latin-American performer. The promoter had taken the girlfriend's word for this actor's singing ability, and the fact that the actor already spoke Spanish clinched the deal.

WIK The Experience Might Be Worth It, Regardless

"That gig took me all over the world," he says. "At the end of the tour, I sent my family tickets to come hear me sing in Carnegie Hall. Two years earlier, I'd left to become an actor in Hollywood, and here I come back with the dream gig—everyone dreams of that—I'm singing in Carnegie Hall in front of my family. Man, that was amazing.

"Here I was living in a hotel in Madrid, all expenses paid for a year. My money was my own (about two grand a week). I'd shoot over to Paris for the weekend. It was amazing. I was living the life. I was in my twenties. Man, life was good."

That's when things took a slight turn.

WIK Work Is Work So Be Happy For Any You Get

"I got back from that gig and I'd get offered these little jobs and I'd be like, 'uh...who...me? Do you know who I am? I just sang at Carnegie Hall.' I felt like these new little jobs were beneath me. I was making two Gs a week a month ago, why should I do your thing for five hundred? That's where I made my mistake. I started thinking there was work that was beneath me."

And pretty soon, there was no work at all. A return to the catering business. A full time job in sales. The cold kiss of reality complete with its funky breath. "But I'll always have that memory of those hotel nights in Madrid."

What would you have done differently?

"I would have taken those little jobs and kept working. I would have realized that the big gig was amazing, but not the norm. I would have remembered that I love to sing and not gotten a big head. Work is work and out here you should to be happy to have any at all. There's no real place for arrogance."

Hyphenate #2 — Actor-Writer-Producer

The next person I interviewed was a veritable almanac of wisdom, someone who came to Hollywood tangentially via background singing. Some ten years ago, while sitting with his partner in their Chicago Police squad car, this former cop says his partner made casual mention of the fact that he'd once had an opportunity to audition as a background singer for Luther Vandross.

"But he was afraid to do it and missed the opportunity. He said it was the biggest regret of his life.

"Then he asked me if there was anything I ever wanted to do that I didn't do. I told him I always wanted to act."

"He asked me, 'So why haven't you?' and I couldn't think of a good answer."

And with that unanswered question buzzing around in his head, the then twenty-nine year old newly married police officer decided to go to Columbia College in Chicago to study theater.

While at Columbia, he auditioned and booked a part in *Barbershop*. Three years later, after saving a little money, he drew down his pension from the Chicago Police Department and moved his family across the country to pursue acting full time.

"My plan was to join the LAPD and rent a house from a friend I knew in Slymar [a suburb in the Valley]. I had some good money saved. I had the house here. It was really nice—a very smooth transition—four bedrooms, a pool. We moved in July 2004. But getting on the LAPD proved crazy. They wanted to interview old girlfriends from twenty years ago—so that didn't happen, but by October, I'd booked my first TV show—an episode of *Cold Case*."

But once again, the acting jobs weren't as consistent as he'd hoped.

"Eventually we had to downgrade from the house to an apartment and I ended up taking a series of jobs—I even worked at Pottery Barn for a while. A friend of mine casts background talent for Honda commercials, so I did that—anything I could.

"About a year later another friend of mine wrote a short film and needed help with a rewrite. I did the rewrite for him and it took first prize in a contest and was later bought by HBO.

"Sometimes you just have to take a chance. I did the numbers. Looking over my taxes, I average about twenty thousand less a year than I made as a cop in Chicago, but I'm doing something I love to do. For me it's worth it."

Since selling the film to HBO, this actor-writer-producer has gone on to appear in *The Shield*, *24*, and *The Unit*, as well as other shows and commercials.

What was your biggest disappointment?

"People I'd seen in movies and thought the world of who turned out to be jerks in real life. That's disappointing. Some people are really cool—I met a few stars who are really cool. But some of the folks I've met who I really admired—some were pretty sleazy."

If you could do it over, is there anything you would have done differently moving here?

"I would have worked one more year and saved more money. I was really shocked at the cost of things here."

If You Can Make It In Any Other Career, Do That Instead of Coming to Hollywood

When I asked what advice he had for anyone considering coming here to break into the business—especially someone who might be looking at giving up a steady job or someone who's married and has a family, he really opened up.

"If there's anything else that you can do [besides be in this business], do it. Don't come here. Because the sacrifice, commitment and focus required is too much. Terrence Howard walked away from acting two times. Careers are twenty years in the making. You gotta be ready to put that kind of time and work in. It's not an overnight thing."

Know Who You Are Before You Get Here

"If you must come here, though, find a place where you can connect to whatever spiritual being you can believe in. You need strength because it's very easy to get distracted. I know people who came here and lost their identity. People who never smoked even a cigarette in their lives and now they're drug addicts. I know people who came here to act and now do porn because they lost their way—young people naïve to the trappings. You really need a strong sense of who you are. I wouldn't wish this lifestyle on anyone."

What other general advice do you have?

WIK Plan On Your Career Taking 20 Years

"Meet as many people as you can. Try to be a help to them. If you write, write at least two hours a day. That can be hard on a family man, like myself, but your family has to understand. Sometimes you just have to go off to Starbucks or the library and get away so you can do your craft. Stay focused on what you want. Don't let anyone tell you 'no.' And you need to have relationships—you need to be in the loop of people who are moving—to get things working in your career. Take Don Cheadle—a few years ago he was jogging around the same park I jog around now, asking people if they knew about any auditions he could do. But then he hooked up with George Clooney. Now he's in that loop."

Being that this actor-writer-producer is a family man, I wanted to get his perspective on how Hollywood and the relentless pursuit of dreams here stresses relationships.

"You need to stay close to home. It can be tempting. It's easy to get off track. Actors in general are desperate—they want in so bad it's hard not to compromise. I've been approached by men, women...you name it. It's not easy on relationships."

It helps to have a spouse who supports your dreams, but in all honesty, I'd say that very help is almost negated simply by having a spouse. In other words, the lifestyle that this interviewee wouldn't wish on anyone, is much better suited to single people. That's just a fact. There's a reason couples here don't stay together. The only exceptions I see to this rule are if both partners are pursuing careers here or if you're independently wealthy. Otherwise marriage fits better after you make it. But during the course of trying to make it happen, being in a relationship is more distraction than benefit.

As this actor-writer-producer says, "If you want to write, you must be selfish until you get it on the page." In its own way, that's true of any pursuit in such a competitive field. Families don't always understand, but if you want success in this business, know that is part of the cost.

Thespians of stage and screen

Actor # 1

 **Create a Business Plan for Your Career**

"Before I came out here, I had a mentor help me develop a business plan for becoming a working actor. If anything, people need to know that they need a plan to become what they want to be. I think the reason I've been successful is because I had that plan and stuck with it," says this 28-year-old working actor who moved to Hollywood a year after graduating from college.

Although inspired to act at thirteen, as a young adult, he had other plans at first.

"I was on a different path—wanted the money—to be the CEO of a company. But in college I tried out for a part and got it. Then I got more."

Next thing he knew he was almost ready to drop out of college altogether. Majoring in finance while spending all his time acting wasn't making any sense. He decided to visit Hollywood and check it out.

"I was even creative with how I came to visit. I had an internship that summer with Frito-Lay in Texas. At the end of the summer they flew us home. I told them I lived in Los Angeles. That's how I got here."

WIK 23 Walk Into Anyone's Office—Talk to Anybody and Don't Be Afraid to Ask Anyone Anything

"I learned that people will talk, promise you anything—things they can't do. When I came out to Hollywood, my friend said he could help me get work, but he couldn't. Still, I just went around everywhere I heard they were holding auditions. I walked into anyone's office and did what I had to do. Ended up meeting a casting agent who let me do background on *The District*. That did it for me. I knew then I could make it as an actor."

That was the summer between his sophomore and junior years in college. And that is when he went back and got his plan together.

"The next year I took a job with Frito-Lay again and saved a good amount of money for a year. I then became a substitute teacher and booked my first real work back east on an HBO series. I was on it for one season—still living with my parents and saving money.

"When the season ended I was told I would receive a call about becoming a contracted character, but no one called. So I figured while I was on a show it was a good time to go to L.A. and try to get an agent. So I did."

Remember, an agent will be happy to sign you if you're already working on a show—they won't turn down the free percentage. Of course, that's when the call came from the series saying they wanted him for another season.

"I told them I had an agent now and they were like, 'What? What'd you go get an agent for?' And everything changed. See, with an agent, there are rules—they couldn't give me the same offer they'd been planning on giving me. The agent wanted more money.

"I sat watching my agent on the phone with the producers of the show talking about, '[Such and such show—a rival series] wants him...' Next thing I knew they flew me out for one more show...and they killed my character.

"Funny how things work out. Because my character got killed, I didn't get typecast like the others on that show—those actors tell me now they can't get any roles except for the kind they played on the show because people see them that way now. That didn't happen to me. I ended up getting a lot of different guest roles. In fact, I got one role on *Without a Trace* that paid as much as I'd made on the HBO series the whole season."

That was fortunate. And shortly thereafter, this actor booked a major role in two motion pictures.

"And that was all part of the plan. I didn't buy a nice car or live in a nice apartment when I moved here. I stayed with one friend for three months, another for six... I held onto my money and really stretched it out so that I could get established."

Since then things have slowed down a bit?

"Yeah, I'm just now starting to come to the end of that original business plan I made with my mentor and I'm thinking of how to grow from here. I'm venturing behind the camera—writing and shooting stuff with friends—trying to find the new angle to acting."

It's a story I've heard often. Actors write their roles so they can play the characters they want to play. The first I remember was Sylvester Stallone who wrote *Rocky* so he could star in it. It worked for him. Vin Diesel did something similar with a documentary about being a mixed-raced actor trying to break into Hollywood—about not really fitting into the types of roles that were being cast. It worked very well for him, too. Even writers have been doing it—trying to make their own films because no one else will—including Tyler Perry, for instance.

What, if anything, would you have done differently in your business plan?

"I would have taken more advantage of my opportunities. I would have talked more with the star actors when I was on set with them. I would have had less fear in those situations. I would have asked them what was their next project and if they could get me on it with them.

"If it's a question you wouldn't mind someone asking you—then ask. Don't make situations worse than they are by being fearful. Actors wouldn't be in this work if they didn't like the attention."

Was there anything you encountered when you got here that you didn't expect?

"I wasn't prepared for the shallowness and phoniness of people—people who don't pay any attention to you until they hear you're on a show—photographers who don't take your picture when you walk by, but later find out who you are and then want to take it. Why can't people just be decent and talk or take a picture regardless?

"It's very hard to tell who's genuinely interested in you versus what you've done. Some of my friends get jaded by that, but I just try to be me in every situation."

Any other advice for people who might be considering taking on this business?

"I'm not too hot on acting school. When I do an audition, I audition against people who went to Yale Drama. It doesn't really matter in this field like it does in other fields—you don't have to have a degree to act. You go up to a casting agent and give them your resume and they say, 'Okay, come audition.' That's it. You don't get the job because you have the best credentials. So have another set of skills to help you in life—like business.

"You have to know acting is for you. You have to have a purpose for what you want to do, not just surface passion. And be grounded in God, because in this business there are so many other made-up gods that will steer you the wrong way."

 Don't Become Part of Anyone's Entourage

"One other thing—don't become part of anyone's entourage. You have to maintain your integrity. I see actors all the time who hang out with directors or other actors, but never get to work with them. They aren't in any films, but they're hanging out. Too many parties means you're too accessible. When they can see you anytime, you're not busy. Be careful what side you show people. Show them your working side more than your party side."

Actor # 2

A young actor could do a lot worse than having his first movie be a role opposite Russell Crowe and Denzel Washington—especially a speaking role with him and Denzel going at it one-on-one—yeah, a lot worse.

Before that opportunity opened up though, this young thespian went a whole year with an agent, auditioning, doing callbacks, and booking absolutely nothing.

His New York hustle included catering, singing telegrams, and getting by with occasional help from his parents. Between his different jobs he pulled in about $500 a week, which was enough to pay his one-third share of rent ($675) for his three-bedroom apartment.

 **Don't Let the Politics Get You Down**

"The most stressing aspect is working really hard and doing the best in the part, but having a bigger 'name' actor take the part. It's the way the politics work here. But I get now that this business isn't about your feelings, it's about making money. At some point it will be you they need for the part."
Struggling has taught him to live "super-frugally" because he doesn't want to be a caterer again.

Coming from New York, what about Hollywood has surprised you?

"I never heard people talking about drugs so casually like, 'We're gonna go do some coke,' like they're going to smoke cigs. I realized it's easy to get off track. Hollywood is like high school [with the pressure to fit in]. You have to know who you are."

What would you suggest for someone looking to make it out here?

WIK Know Your Type—Know How You're Seen by Other People Stay Up On Your Craft

"Self marketing. Know your type. Know how you're seen by other people and know your market. Know what roles you should be going for and be able to see yourself clearly in those roles. Think about how badly you want it, and know that it will take so much more than you think. You have to compete with everyone else who wants in. So stay up on your craft. Go over-and-above in putting yourself out there."

"Things have gone very well for me since I've moved here. I've booked a couple plays. I won an award. I'm living off a bit of savings from *Law and Order* and waiting on my residuals from *American Gangster* to show up. I still can't splurge, but I'm making it."

Comedian-Writer

This next artist was a tad more jaded than others. He's achieved great success by writing for some of the biggest African American comedians in the field, producing TV series, writing for sitcoms and performing standup comedy. More than for any other interviewee, I feel a need to make sure it's clear that his opinions are his own, and not mine. Statements he makes are based on his experiences and cannot be verified independently.

"I read a book once entitled *The Writer Got Screwed*, by Brooke Wharton, which paints a rich picture of exploitation in Hollywood. It does seem to be true that writers often get screwed more than others do in this town. That's no doubt because, in Hollywood, writers give their thoughts and words to others to say and perform. And it may well be true that some people believe actors just make up their lines as they go along. That's certainly what people believe of comedians.

"You write a joke for some TV or radio personality... you're making that person look good. You're making them look smarter than they really are. People see them as clever or wise and they reap all types of benefits from that, but it's amazing how few appreciate it, how they'll just take the credit and forget that you wrote it for them."

This writer feels that it wouldn't be so bad if he were at least paid well for the work.

"Some guys want to low-ball you. This guy comes to meet me for lunch driving an S-Class Benz and wearing a $10,000 watch—it kills me how folk always gotta have a flashy hobby like expensive watches or cars or shoes—I know how much it costs because I was with him when he bought it. He wants me to punch up his new script. I give him the cheap rate--$1,500. I should have been charging him $5,000 or more, but I call myself helping him out. I never heard from him again. He spent more than that on his shoes, but he doesn't want to pay me to help him get his script right.

"People's priorities can be all out of whack. There are very few stars that have a sense of balance. They tend to believe their own hype.

"[A famous comedian]'s agent came to me and told me, '[the comedian] is about to host [a nationwide awards show] and he wants you to write some jokes for him.' I said, 'Cool, how much am I getting?' Know what this guy said to me? He said, 'We're not paying anything, we figure it should be an honor to write for [him].' I said, 'Is it an honor to represent him or do you get paid?' Son of a bitch is full of shit...An honor? Who's he think he is? It'd be an honor for me to write for Chris Rock, Dave Chappelle, Eddie Murphy—and I'd write for them for free—but those cats wouldn't ask someone to write for them for free because they respect the craft."

Learn How To Buddy Hustle

"If you're a writer, you better learn to buddy hustle—nurture relationships. That's my biggest problem. I haven't learned how to navigate around people's insecurities and cheapness. It's not enough to make someone look funnier or smarter than they are. I come from back east where work is rewarded based on how hard or how well you work, not on ass kissing. That's just not true in Hollywood. The guys who show up and hang out everywhere with all the new talent that comes down the pipe, those are the guys working now. I care, but I can't be phony telling people they're all this or that. I feel I need to be honest."

Keep Your Opinions to Yourself

"But in Hollywood, you're better off keeping your opinions to yourself. Stars are insecure and hold genuine opinions against you. So give 'em the fake shit.

"Honesty just doesn't fly. Stars want 'yes' men. Even though they need someone bringing the real—like Eddie [Murphy] back when he did *Raw*. Eddie needed someone telling him he can't go on stage wearing tight leather pants and a glove with a ring on it and a lace scarf. Someone shoulda told him only Prince can get away with that shit, not a [n-word] from Brooklyn.

"Real friends give you boundaries. When you don't have boundaries, it creeps into your choices in movies and life. If nobody around you tells you the truth, you end up doing all kinds of stupid shit."

WIK ⓣ Always Be Writing —Every Day

"In terms of the craft though, I tell people to always be writing—every day. When you're writing, comedy that is, be funny and relatable."

WIK ⓣ Once You Work Three Years, You're Out of Touch

"But what happens out here is, if you work steady for three years, you just lose touch with reality. You make too much money. Your relationships become superficial. You can't be real and be yourself. You're surrounded by superficial people and you become superficial too. Then your writing starts to suffer. And once you've become successful, the yes men you've surrounded yourself with are afraid to critique you honestly—so they let you keep going down the wrong path and you fall off."

WIK ⓣ Tell Minorities to Get Ready to Deal with Racism

"The way it works in Hollywood is this—there's a black comedian [the network] wants to build a show around. So they send white show runners to watch his standup and then they try to develop a show based on a twenty-minute routine. That's why black shows come off stereotypical or stupid, playing to the same lame premises.

"That show runner hires his college buddies to write with him. These guys don't know anything about that comedian's world or his life—just twenty minutes of jokes.

"John Bowman ran *Martin* and filled the room with black writers and the show was the most original and funniest new black comedy ever. Why was that not duplicated?

"Larry Wilmore [a black writer] got screwed over with *The Bernie Mac Show*. He created and ran it so well the first two years that he won an Emmy. But they fired Larry dirty—they did it over the trades [newspapers—*Variety* and *Hollywood Reporter*] in public. Then they bring in a showrunner that used to write on *Friends* like that's a big deal. So what? Everyone wrote for *Friends*. Next thing you know, they've got Bernie hiding under the table on Thanksgiving eating a turkey leg like a coon on some chicken—same tired race jokes. The show wasn't funny anymore after Larry left. I love Bernie, we go way back. I just wish he'd stood up for Larry and not let that happen.[7]

"But that's how it is here. Black writers get pigeonholed in black comedy only. But still, because of the buddy hustle, a corny white guy has a better shot getting a job writing even on a black show than a black guy does."

One of the stories I heard from other writers happened about the time that *Grey's Anatomy* got picked up by ABC. A talented African-American writer named Shonda Rhimes created the show. The story goes that when she went to interview writers for the show, she was surprised that none of the writers she met with were minorities. When she asked the network and agencies why, she was told none were called because she had not specifically requested they be included.

Obviously, if the only way a show can be staffed with minority writers is that creators and showrunners specifically ask for them, the majority of shows will not have minority representation among the writers. Via extrapolation, very little diversity will be seen in show topics or characters, and stereotypes are likely to prevail. As is the nature of television, where only experienced writers are invited to create new shows, the future show

---

7 This interview was conducted in May 2008, prior to the unexpected death of Bernie Mac. He and his amazing talent will be missed.

runners and creators will continue to perpetuate this problem.

If you're a minority writer, it's just something to be aware of. If you're a majority writer, it's something to be sensitive to.

Larry David is one showrunner who seems to have figured this out with his new show *Curb Your Enthusiasm*. David created *Seinfeld*, a show set in New York City, which ran on NBC for nine years (and likely will be in syndication forever). One criticism of that hilarious show was that it featured no significant minority characters, with the exception of occasional bit characters like Jackie Chiles, played by Phil Morris. Over the course of its run, Seinfeld had numerous critics asking how a show set in one of the most diverse cities in the world could have so few minorities on it.

David's new show is set in L.A. and Santa Monica. David manages to have minorities in nearly every episode, and he's funnier than ever. What's more, the humor and characters are believable and inoffensive even when dealing with sensitive subjects because, as the show is partly improvised, the actors are writers and actually do make up some of it as they go along.

Of course, Larry David is a genius.

Musicians

Multi-Platinum Music Producer

Of all the people I interviewed, I've known this guy the longest. Blessed with an amazing musical talent, he's produced music for some of the biggest names in hip-hop and his work has contributed to numerous gold- and platinum-selling CDs. His insights into the music business are exceptional and will profit anyone looking to get into that business.

 **Don't Rely Solely on Your Dream**

"One of the biggest pitfalls I've seen is people relying totally on their dream and not having a job in the meantime. Those people run into the wall really fast when they realize all that glitters isn't gold—especially if it takes a couple years. They get jaded and if they come from another city, they pack up and go back.

"People come here naïve. I did. I just wanted to work. I saw my friends getting killed back home and I was just happy to be alive. I was doing all this work and wasn't getting paid anything. I didn't care. I just liked seeing something go from conception to a finished product."

WIK Go Where Things Are Happening in Your Field

"I was in Atlanta at the time and there was nothing poppin' there at the time like it is now. My friend got assigned to Death Row Records and came out here to L.A., so I came out with him.

"When guys would go out to clubs, I'd be at home on the drum machine. I saw so many guys get messed up with drugs and girls.

"The first job I got I was offered 'five' for some beats. I would have done it for free, but I was like, 'Wow, $500 for doing what I love to do?' I was happy. Turned out to be $5,000."

WIK Know Your Worth

"That was my biggest mistake. I didn't know what I was worth. I didn't understand what people got paid for doing what I was doing, so I made some mistakes."

WIK Keep Your "Publishing"! It's Mailbox Money

"Probably the biggest mistake was signing away my publishing. I had a number one album on radio at the time. I got offered $150,000 for fifty percent of my publishing. I didn't know what it was worth. I signed exclusive for pennies. I was happy-go-lucky. I was worth much more, but I didn't know. My album was headed platinum. Everybody else knew, but not me.

"I not only could have gotten more money, I could have chosen not to sign exclusively. If I hadn't signed exclusive, I would have worked with a lot more people and not felt boxed in and I would have owned my own publishing."

What is "publishing?"

"That's the most important thing a music producer wants to keep. It's how you get paid after-the-fact. It's royalties. It's also how you leverage your negotiations later when your stuff gets remixed, reused.

"Companies use publishing to build their catalog of songs and sell those catalogs for hundreds of millions of dollars. Remember when Michael Jackson got portions of the Beatles' catalog? Even today, Michael gets paid every time you hear a Beatles song. Royalties keep going and going. Instead, I got put on a contract with a signing bonus and salary. I got paid $20,000 to $25,000 a song."

Apparently royalties show up in places you don't even realize.

"Performance royalties work like this—you get paid every time your song is played anywhere. They play it ten times in L.A., fifteen times in Connecticut, eight times in New York—that's money.

"In TV, for every cue you do, it's a performance royalty. I did some scoring for a TV show. They paid me only twenty-five percent of what I made doing other stuff. I didn't even realize how it worked in TV. The show I did went into syndication. Now I may have done forty-seven music cues in one show. That's like having forty-seven singles going at the same time when it's played in syndication. Every station around the country pays for each music cue each time it's played. They got me on those royalties, too. So you gotta know what you're worth. But not so much that you kill deals over it."

WIK Sometimes the Opportunity is Worth More Than Being Paid Right

"I've seen that happen, too. It's a balance. You have to know enough not to get raped, but not demand so much that you cut yourself out of deals. Sometimes the opportunity is worth more than you being paid right. And, if you can't get along [because you're worried about being cheated] it's hard to work with you. I've seen that... guys who you know are thinking about something besides what they're being paid to be there doing."

WIK Companies Know How to Use You

But even if you're aware of what your value is and you understand the money involved, you must still be vigilant in dealing with people and companies that have been in this business for years. They have so many tricks up their sleeves.

"They know how to use you. When someone has never had anything and then they get something, they lose their minds. They lose loyalties and all. Companies know these guys sit around watching BET all day thinking they're ready to blow up. So companies cater to egos. They bring up conversations around Artist A about Artist B, and what Artist B got paid, in order to get Artist A to lower his standards. 'Such and such made a song like...' Next thing you know, Artist A is doing it too, just like they wanted him to.

"There are even companies that sign artists as a tax write-off. Their album never comes out and the artist doesn't know what's up.

"Where Artist A messes up is when he lowers his standards and does stuff he doesn't like because there's a hit out by Artist B and the label wants Artist A to do something like it. Artist A might try to do a hybrid or something—kind of like Artist B, but not fully. Artist A figures he'll do it to please the company. But then it blows up and Artist A is stuck. He can't get out of it after that—he's pigeonholed. He thought he could jump on and back off again, but he can't." So his whole career becomes doing stuff he doesn't even like. Wow.

I saw a special about the R&B group TLC one day in which the ladies of the group claimed they were in debt to their label even when they had number one songs on the radio. How does that happen?

"Artists hunger to look good. They get advances from the label before their album comes out and they don't realize those advances get recouped. But there's other stuff that's recouped too. A company might spend $600,000 in publicity, $1,000,000 in the studio making the album—and on top of that pay the artists $300,000 in advances. It all ads up and an artist can end up being in the hole before they even come out.

"There's this old saying from Robert Kiyosaki, 'If your outgo exceeds your income, then your upkeep will be your downfall.' Now that's truth.

"I worked with one company where all was gravy wherever you wanted to go. You fly first class. There's a driver at the airport to take you in a limo wherever you want. He waits for you for eleven hours while you're in the studio. But none of that is free. You're paying for that. You're paying for him sitting in the car reading a book."

Tell us a little about music videos. I understand a lot of the stuff you see in videos isn't real or is just rented. What's that about? I thought it was all about keeping it real?

 **Music Videos Are Advertisements**

"You know, people don't think about it, but videos, photo shoots, interviews—it may look like they're fronting, but it's all an ad.

"If DUB Magazine loans a car for a video, that artist is doing an ad for DUB. DUB is gonna make it look good. Fans are then gonna wanna buy DUBs. Everybody is making money off the audience. Videos are a projection of how they want to be seen. And, in general, everyone wants their video to shine above other videos."

And he's absolutely right. I went online to dubmag.net and there they are. All the stars in their DUB cars. It's funny because DUB makes rims, but the cars have DUB on the license plates. There was a video of David Beckham driving a Rolls-Royce Drophead through Beverly Hills. They report it as "David Beckham spotted in Beverly Hills in his DUB Drophead with his three sons," but the video they attached is obviously set up—cut and edited—front shots, side shots, rear shots. They grain it up to make it look as if some tourist filmed it, but it's professional.

Beckham could not drive through Beverly Hills with the top and all his windows down and not have paparazzi jumping in his car at every stop light. And why would his license plate say "DUB"? So people will want to go buy DUB rims.

I hadn't thought about it, but it is true that these artists aren't competing with the audience—saying they look better than the audience or drive nicer cars than them; they're competing with other artists.

"And sure they rent homes and show them on *MTV Cribs*. But if you're in town for a month, it's cheaper to rent a house than to stay at the Four Seasons.

"Many times you see a brand new artist with a bunch of jewelry on, it's fake, but you can't tell on TV. Or maybe Jacob and Company sends over a watch for them to wear for the shoot. They can't turn it down. The label wants you to look good. The artists get to look cool in the video. They have to give it back after the shoot, but nobody knows that.

"Another thing...if you're really successful or on your way up, you're working or on the road ninety percent of your time. It really doesn't make any sense to buy a Rolls-Royce Phantom and have it sitting somewhere and never drive it. But they want to appear like everyone else, so they get one for the shoot."

And it must be working because suddenly there are more Bentleys and Phantoms on the street than I've ever seen before. They used to be rare. Not anymore. Bentleys seem to be the new Mercedes.

I actually saw a Bugatti Veyron on the bed of a delivery truck rushing down the Hollywood Freeway. I was surprised there wasn't a cover on the million-dollar car, but I guess not, if the goal is for it to be seen. No doubt it was destined for someone's video. Didn't notice if it said "DUB" on the license plate, but I imagine it may well say it soon.

On a slight side note, seeing the Bugatti was particularly funny to me because in one of my scripts, (which is about four years old), the main character's brother purchases a Bugatti Veyron (the most expensive production car in the world) for a million dollars, and sells it six months later for two and a half million. When people read the script, they didn't know what the car was. My manager joked about the feasibility of producing a film that had a million dollar car in it. But put the right rapper in the role of the brother and you can get the car for free.

Talk to me about the future of the music business considering all the downloading that's going on nowadays.

"The future of the industry is definitely digital. Mom and pop stores are headed out—even the bigger chains are too. It's just more accessible to buy from the privacy of your home. Plus you get to preview songs and only buy the ones you like. It's cheaper.

"File sharing is hurting a little, but they're crunching down on file sharing. Nothing stops hand-to-hand bootleggers. Much of that comes from the inside—folks working inside the studio steal copies of new music and sell it for a few grand. It's hard to track that because more than one person has access and companies can't tell who's leaking it.

"Technology makes it where you don't have to know how to do something to get on. T-Pain can't sing, but he uses a machine, an Autotone, to stay in key. They used to just use those to help singers stay clear in their upper registers, but the way he figured to use it...it wasn't meant to be used that way, but it works.

"What's most wild about technology like that is now you have big acts, like Fifty Cent, trying to sound like smaller acts, like T-Pain. It was never that way in the past.

"As far as the sound...the South is having its time. For the longest it was East Coast/West Coast and nobody paid any attention to the South. Now the South has it and they ain't letting go.

"Kids don't know any better. I was listening to a hip-hop station the other day and they said they were going to play some 'old school.' Then they played Ja Rule. I was like, 'What? Ja Rule? Ja Rule is old school now?'"

So he is. After all, when Ja Rule came out (in 1999) there was no such thing as downloading music (Napster came out later that year and took a minute to spread) and no such thing as an iPod. Those came out two years later. It's been almost ten years since Ja Rule and nearly fifteen since Tupac and Biggie.

Gold Record Selling Male Singer

This artist would be one of the three most recognizable names on this list, if the names were published—he's a genuine star. Although you don't have to be a star to make it big in Hollywood, I was interested in his road and what he's learned along the way.

WIK Watch Your Money Yourself

"Number one on my list would be this...if you're an adult, you have to learn to run your own life. I was told I needed someone to handle my money. Bad move.

"I admit that when I started, the technology didn't exist for me to track my money like it does now. But today there's no excuse. I needed to know how to interview someone to be my business manager. Fees lead to debt."

WIK Your Business Manager Needs to Be a Mentor, Too

"A good business manager needs to be a mentor, too. He should be teaching you about your money and how it's invested and why. My business manager had no wealth plan, no savings plan, no 'buy a house' plan. And when you deal with a large firm, you can't see how your money will be handled—how do you know how your accountant handles their own money if you're dealing with a big firm? If there are areas in your accountant's life that are out of control, they will be out of control in your life as well.

"Truth be told, I have other friends with less success than I've had that have better financial stability because they had better advisors.

"One meeting I had... I was introduced to a business manager by my agent. My agent tells him I'm not like other young singers [just trying to buy flashy toys]. This guy actually says to my face 'He's not like that... *yet.*' The guy had no respect for me as a man, much less a businessman."

The implication is that if he's willing to say that to your face, imagine what he willing to do behind your back. "Exactly. People take stars' money and think nothing of it."

I asked him to talk a bit about what frustrations he's had in the business—things he didn't expect.

"There's a lot of pressure to do music that other people wanted me to do that I didn't want to do. I was part of so many deals that I didn't have any autonomy. It felt good [in some ways] because it meant [the record execs] were thinking about me. As an artist, you're affected by the politics."

That sounds a lot like what the music producer described. And again, politics. We've seen how it works in film. How does politics play out in the music business?

WIK The Industry Is Far More Political Than Creative

"You don't get a shot because your music is great. You get a shot because someone likes you or thinks you'll make money for them. Hits are made and paid for."

When he said that, a bell rang in my head and suddenly a whole host of things made sense. There are groups and singers and other artists that really make me wonder if I've lost my mind. I honestly can't comprehend why they are famous or successful, yet they sell out concerts and they seem to stay perpetually in the media, to the point where it really feels like their daddy owns the network or something. Now I know.

What other things does he wish he knew?

WIK Don't Feel Guilty for Your Success

"If you have success you can feel guilty for it. You spend $250 at a spa or just the fact that you can go and buy a $200,000 car when someone in your family has a need... that can mess you up. But giving away money to everyone can mess you up too. And giving people money sometimes cripples them because they start to think they have more than they do.

"One day a friend sat me down and told me to ask this question, 'Would they (the people who ask him for money) have done what you did to get success?' And when I thought about all I'd done... sleeping on couches, catching trains in the middle of the night, watching people's kids for them, singing on people's albums for free.... That freed me from a lot of guilt."

WIK People Take Stars' Money and Think Nothing of It

"I still help folk out, but I'm much more hard-nosed about it. I ask a few more questions. It's crazy when you find out they just went to get their hair and nails done and bought a new suit and shoes and now they're short on the rent. That's not a money problem, that's a priority problem. If I help them out, they'll just keep having the same priorities."

Like he said before, people take stars' money and think nothing of it. Apparently that doesn't just apply to the reps that charge you fees.

"It's like that for pro athletes too. Those boys really get it from everybody they know."

That's another book. My niece was once engaged to a professional football player and I was always amazed at how controlled those guys' lives are. As is true with many successful folk in Hollywood, agents (10%)

recommend their managers (10-20%), their lawyers (5%), their real estate agents, their lenders, their accountants, their bankers—all of whom have their hands in the athletes' pockets.

Now to whom do you imagine those professional service people are most beholden? Athletes come and go, but a good agent relationship is worth ten or more athlete-client referrals. You can rest assured their allegiance is to the agent, not the client. Keep that in mind when you become successful.

"I've lost tons of money to accountants and people masquerading as accountants. We really need to do a better job of watching our own money."

Grammy Nominated Gold Selling Female Singer

This artist told me the story of growing up in a musical family and having a love for singing. Her family, however, believed it wasn't the love of singing that she lacked, but the capability to sing. "My mom brought me a tape recorder so I could hear how bad I sang. I didn't care how I sounded. I just always loved singing for singing."

That love of singing rewarded her with her first record deal at the age of nineteen. She obviously got considerably better with time.

 **Failures Can Become Tickets to Your Success**

"I remember crying while signing the contract. I didn't know what I was signing. Some friends in San Diego knew a lady that worked at Warner Bros. so they signed me before taking me to her. I recorded a whole album that never came out. But the good thing is that that failed album became my demo. I was twenty-three by the time I actually got an album released."

WIK 23:What They Know

Until then, she honed her singing skills singing in clubs in San Diego and various festivals.

"In my first contract, [the people repping me] took eighty percent of my publishing. [The contract] heavily favored them. It was so bad, in fact, that the record company couldn't make any money, so they had to buy those guys out and give me a better contract," she laughs. "People use you. It's more about business than music. For me, it was mostly about people trying to use my body and that I presented myself [as a sex symbol] than how I sang."

WIK The Casting Couch is Very Real

According to this Grammy nominated singer, the concept of the casting couch[8] is very real in the music business. "Oh, it's not just actors, but singers as well. Men wanted to sleep with me. Women who had slept with certain men got [certain benefits to their careers]. But it's not just men—women want sex from women, too. There are all types of promises of helping you out if you'll lower your standards."

You've had great success in this business. Imagine you're talking to a group of young people looking to make it as singers in Hollywood. What would tell them? What things, if any, do you wish you knew before you got here? My pen could barely keep up with the advice she began dispensing.

---

8   The **casting couch** *is a euphemism for a sociological phenomenon that involves the trading of sexual favors by an aspirant, apprentice employee, or subordinate to a superior, in return for entry into an occupation, or for other career advancement within an organization. Careers which are highly desirable and traditionally difficult to break into, such as the movie, television and music industries, have been the subject of casting couch stories in popular culture.*

WIK  You Need Good Representation and to Know How to Represent Yourself, Too.

"First, I'd tell them they really need to get good representation—good management and a lawyer they can trust. But on top of that you have to know how to represent yourself online—the Internet has really changed how artists relate to their audience."

Speaking of the Internet, you have a MySpace page, do you go on there and talk to fans yourself?

"I used to. I used to be more personal, but it can be very emotional. People say painful things online. Some people come online just to say negative things to hurt you. I was in tears a few times, so I don't do it anymore. People can be very mean."

I have to admit that that is something I'd never thought about. Whenever I saw artists' sites on MySpace, I always thought the artists were constantly adored by fans and that the artists likely went online purely for the ego boost. I had not thought about the possibility of hate posts.

I apologized for interrupting her train of thought and asked her to continue with her advice.

"I'd tell them to be prepared. You really need to work on your craft to be excellent. There's not a lot of real musicianship—quality voices. Lots of folk can shake their tail but they can't sing."

WIK  Be Prepared to Be Rejected

"You also need to be prepared to be rejected. You have to know that what someone says [about you] doesn't determine who you are. If you believe everything they say about you when you're hot and on top of the charts, what happens when they're done with you—are you what they say you are then? You have to know who you are from within."

WIK Many People In This Industry Are Users

"Remember that people are users in this industry—they'll use you to get money or they'll try to use you physically. This industry is about sex and people want that from you. There are a lot of drugs here, too. You have to represent yourself right to keep yourself from being used. Women can be used more than men. For men, it's their music, pride and ego, but for women, it's music, pride, ego and body. You can't let them abuse and misuse you. You need to be business savvy to know good deals from bad ones."

WIK If You Don't Motivate Yourself, No One Else Will

"Here's something people don't realize: You have to be self-motivating. You have to get up and do what you have to do when you don't feel like it. No one's going to make you do it. You have to take care of yourself— exercise and practice singing. You have to do interviews when you don't feel like talking."

"You also have to protect yourself from overdoing it. If you have family, it's tough. This business is easier for single people. You have to be fairly self-consumed. There's a lot of travel. You have to be out and about—being seen, going to clubs. Networking."

WIK  Parties Aren't All About Fun

You talk about networking and going to clubs. Please talk about parties. You see these entertainment shows and there are always all these celebrities at all these parties and they seem to go on all the time.

"Here's the thing with parties. The record labels want you seen. You have to go to parties to be seen. If you're not invited to a certain big party, then you might not be a 'who'. But if you're at too many parties, your value goes down. If you don't go to some of the more important parties, you suffer—not because of vindictiveness, but because you miss opportunities. You meet people at parties—the new hot producer or whatever—and he might think to do a song with you. Or there's someone who has a song they've written that's perfect for you—it could be your next big hit. Other times people aren't aware that you've released a new album. You have to let them know. Parties help connect you because, even though someone is in the industry, they don't always know what's going on with you."

What other things do you wish you knew?

"Be prepared to do your best, but expect the worst. And here's something to think about in this business... Whatever your weakness or vice is, if you become successful, it will present itself on a platter. If you're not used to getting what you want, you will get it—just be sure you know what you want. If you're sleeping spiritually, you'll be eaten alive.

"You have to know who you are or you'll be lost—wondering how you got [in that situation] and embarrassing yourself. Remember that ultimately [happiness and success] is about what you think of yourself. You need people around you who will speak truth to you and keep you grounded."

I'd heard that from a few different people. It seems to be a consistent warning that, when success comes your way, there is a tendency to lose one's center of focus. I know from personal experience that you can lose your focus when success doesn't come as you planned. But as this artist says, it's important to stay focused always because, "If you're not going up, where are you going?"

Any final words?

"Yes. I would tell anyone coming into this business to remember that being wise means manipulating the situation, not people."

I thanked her for the interview and for her poignant and honest insights, then she added this little bonus: "You can use my name. I don't care." I thanked her, but said I wanted to be consistent.

TV Star

I debated with myself over where I should include this final interviewee. He is a multi-award winning actor of both stage and screen. He is a thirty-year veteran of acting with twenty of those years here in L.A. in both feature films and television. Recently, however, he broke through to the big time and is now one of the highest paid actors in Hollywood, commanding over $100,000 per episode for his work.

My initial thought was to include him in the actor section, but it seemed to me that the insights he offered from his mature perspective might overshadow some of the information that followed. So I decided to include his advice here, at the end of this section.

Over the course of three phone interviews, all in between set changes on his show, he spoke to me for an hour. The first two interviews concluded with a knock on his trailer door followed by a voice saying, "They are ready for you, sir, whenever you're ready." At the end of his next sentence, he would apologize for having to interrupt the interview and promise to return the call at an exact time. Both times he returned at that exact time. I mention this because this was part of my impression of him. He was excellent in his discipline and amazingly humble and courteous.

I couldn't resist doing the math though. At his published salary, the three twenty-minute interviews he gave me over those two days works out to approximately $2,083 dollars worth of his time. When they pay you that much, I suppose you should hurry back to the set without delay. $2,083 an hour—Wow! To quote him, "That'll be me one day." And maybe that will be you, too!

Of all the interviews, this one actually seemed to give the most credence to the concept of chance and circumstance.

"I never planned on being an actor. A friend wanted me to audition in college. I did it to impress the young lady I was dating at the time. I got the role because I was the only one there. But once I got a taste of acting, it was like eating peanuts—I couldn't just have one.

"Did some theater locally, moved to New York and did a few soaps and some Broadway. About 1990, my manager got a job in California and wanted to take some of his clients. He asked me to come with, so I did. Didn't fare well at first. I finally booked a recurring role on [a huge sitcom at the time]."

WIK L.A. is All About Business

"L.A. is all about business. It's really governed by a different master than New York. It's not really who you know, but being in the right place at the right time. It's about being steadfast. You come in, do the job. Most folk who make it just get lucky. They have the look [the casting director] is looking for—so the [casting director] takes whatever talent [the actor] has. Most times what [the actor] has lends itself more to celebrity than talent.

"L.A. is not really about acting. TV is a producer's medium. Film is a director's medium. Actors have no real control. Sometimes you do a take and you think you did it well and the director wants you to do it again a different way. So you do. They may use the take that isn't how you wanted to do it. But it's their decision. Once you understand that and know your place, you're cool."

"Most people who give you jobs have no idea what they are doing. It's a business run by businessmen. They have a business degree, not a theater degree. These are the people who run Hollywood."

WIK Acting is One of the Most Unglamorous Jobs There Is

"Young actors don't realize this, but acting is the one of the most unglamorous jobs. It's one of the most fickle. There are some great rewards. But this is a business. The things you think they look at, they don't. It's really a war of attrition. If you stick around long enough, you'll work. Some very talented actors don't work. I consider myself blessed.

"If you come here to be a star or celebrity—looking for all the perks and accoutrements—then you're in it for the wrong reasons because you really have no control over those things.

"There are 120,000 SAG (Screen Actor's Guild) members. At any given time, 85% of them are out of work. The average salary of a SAG member is less than $10,000 a year. Eighteen to 20% fall into star roles and earn serious money. Others are just trying to make at least $7,500 this year so they can qualify for their health and medical benefits. Less than one percent get into the million dollar and double digit million dollar realm."

That really put the reality into perspective for me. I couldn't resist asking him how it made him feel to be one of the chosen few. I wondered if he ever felt guilty?

WIK Everyone Has An Equal Shot at the Gig

"No, I don't feel guilty. Everyone has an equal shot at the gig. You have to go in with the mindset that this is what I want to do and how I make my living. Casting directors know when you walk in who's going to get the job.

"In New York I worked for car fare. I'm a thirty-year overnight success. I have dear friends who haven't worked in years, but I can't worry about why [they haven't and I have]. I can't [afford to] put that in my spirit.

"For three and a half years I was in that place. If it weren't for friends and my wife, I wouldn't have made it. My wife was working as a background singer and traveling a great deal. I took the role of rearing our daughter for two or three years while she made our living. You can start to question what you're doing wrong and what's going on. I would do well on an audition, but couldn't get to the next level. My agent kept pushing me. Friends and family kept pushing me.

"I remember being in Gelson's Market with only a couple of bucks in my pocket and seeing some successful celebrity. I'd daydream about what their life was like. I just fixed the idea in my mind, 'That will be me one day.' I was being tempered."

 ## Marriage Can Work if Your Spouse Understands

I asked him, as I had asked other interviewees, if he felt it was easier being married or single while trying to make things happen in Hollywood.

"Marriage was good for me, but then she was in the business, too. She understood what I was going through. It was hard at times. I had some single friends who resorted to destructive behaviors. I didn't. Of course, it wasn't in my nature either. But talking things out with my wife really helped."

What are some of the keys to making it?

 ## Whenever You Audition, Leave an Impression

"Give the casting director a different take that's better than anyone coming before or after you. Even if you don't get the job, you must leave an impression. The main thing is to stay focused on what you came to do.

Glean something from every audition. Ask your agent what [the casting director] thought.

"I first started getting guest star roles, then I started getting recurring spots. If folk like you, they keep you in mind for other things. One audition can lead to another."

WIK Along With Hard Work, Luck is a Very Real Part of Success Here

"I was lucky to hook into good shows. [Television producer] Steven Bochco became a fan and booked me in numerous *NYPD Blues*, *Beverly Hills 90210* and other shows. Finding the right groups and people [to help you along] helps, but so does having the right work ethic—show up on time; do your job; and be reliable, etc.

"A lot has to do with timing."

It was refreshing to hear him credit the element of luck for some of his success. The number of extremely talented people in Hollywood versus the few who actually make it to that one percent is evidence that luck has a definite role to play.

What other advice does he have?

WIK Trust Your Intuition

"I want to say it this way, and I hope you get what I mean, but don't take anyone's advice. Your intuition will steer you right. Come prepared. Understand they look at it as a business. If you do, you won't be disappointed by rejection.

"Some come because they were told in high school they were talented—

it's not just about that. You need to train. I would go to NY and train in theater first. Theater gives you grounding and discipline and teaches you how to work—how to act in an ensemble. You must share a stage with other actors. It's not just you.

"For people looking to come to Hollywood—if you're looking for celebrity, you need to look into doing something else. If you're just seeking fame, you won't find it. This must be your life's work.

"This is a microwave generation and [young people] want [success] fast. But it takes hard work and sacrifice and that must take precedence above anything else."

If you have a desire to enter this business, do it. By all means, follow your dreams. But make sure to give yourself the best chance possible by gleaning from the insights of these successful Hollywood artists.

I thank each of them for their time and honesty. I have to admit that I've not often thought of the struggle successful stars have grappled with to get to their place on the world stage. I think I've come to understand now that all the struggles we go through are just part of the process of becoming ready—or being tempered—for that eventual role.

Part IV:

Bliss

"It's never too late to be what you might have been."
—Mary Ann Evans (aka George Eliot)

"Dreams come true; without that possibility, nature would not incite us to have them."
—John Updike

"Focusing your life solely on making a buck shows a certain poverty of ambition. It asks too little of yourself. Because it's only when you hitch your wagon to something larger than yourself that you realize your true potential."
—Barack Obama

Conclusion:
The Lesson from Cherry

I mentioned my oldest sister Cherry at the beginning of this book. She was the person who ignited my desire to learn to write thirty years ago when she took me to her job at the Cleveland Electric Illuminating Company.

Three weeks before I finished the first draft of this book, Cherry passed away from a sudden heart attack at the age of fifty-five. Her passing was a shock to everyone who knew her.

I was in the middle of writing this book and had already included her influence in my writing life in the introductory chapters.

I bring Cherry up because, in so many ways, we were opposites. I was ten years old when she took me to her job. She was twenty-five. I am the baby of my family, and she was the oldest. Thirty years later, she still worked for the same company. I once changed jobs ten times in a single year. Every morning Cherry rose before sunrise to go to work, and since I moved to Hollywood, I've usually gone to bed so late that she'd already awakened to start her day in Cleveland. Year after year she endured the constant threat of lay-offs and terminations. I don't think I've ever even thought about being fired from a job.

Like our father before her, who'd worked for forty years at Republic Steel (which he referred to as his hell) before he retired (his heaven) for fifteen years, Cherry looked forward to retiring and enjoying the remainder of her years in comfort. She was due to retire this year.

Eighty-five is the magic number at her company. Once age plus years of service equals eighty-five, an employee is eligible for retirement.

I guess in some ways Cherry's retirement was a little like my wife's journey on *Pyramid*—just because you make it doesn't mean you win.

Cherry absolutely hated every one of her thirty years at that company. But she endured it for that eventual day when she would leave it behind and live off of her life of sacrifice. But that day never came for her.

I believe that if Cherry had known that she would die at fifty-five, she would have lived her life quite differently. The presumption that we will have the time to pursue dreams at some point in the future is not guaranteed. I think it's important to make sure that our right nows have a good dose of dream life in them.

I did follow my bliss to bankruptcy. I've had my share of regrets. I've yet to see the success in this business I would have liked to see by my seventh year here. No doubt about it, it's been very hard at times. But the joy of doing something I love now, rather than hoping to do it "someday" does make it worth it.

I know Cherry lived under a lot of stress related to the daily pressures of a job she hated. I'm quite sure that the heart attack she suffered was partly if not mostly the result of suppressed dreams beneath the weight of thirty years of delayed gratification. Even so, it seems so unfair.

And yet, why do we believe those who tell us that we'll live to be a hundred—that we have plenty of time? The only real time we have is the present. Medicine may be advancing, but so are the numbers of things that stress us, pollute our bodies, and kill us.

A short time ago prescription drugs were discovered in the water supplies of a number of major cities. Not just human prescriptions like heart medications and anti-depressants, but dog and cat meds too. They even found sex hormones in San Francisco's water. We may live to be one hundred, but who's to say we'll be the same people when we get there, or that we'll want to be alive in that world?

My granddad lived to be ninety-six years old, and he ran his general store in Snowhill, Alabama until he was ninety-four. He loved that store and his place in the community. Gramps had promised his oldest son, my uncle Bubba, that he could have the store when Gramps retired. Bubba finally got his chance to be the boss when he was seventy-seven.

That's what happens when you love what you do. You keep doing it, you live long, and you die when they take it away from you.

My dad, on the other hand, hated his job in the steel mill and couldn't wait to retire. At least he got fifteen years of retired bliss—that is, when he wasn't running to the doctor or when he wasn't in the hospital.

Sis died at fifty-five. Of course she enjoyed her day-to-day time with her daughter, pets, family and friends along with the occasional vacation, etc., but she got none of the bliss for which she delayed gratification until retirement. The way I see it, I don't have the time to put off my bliss. If we're not following our bliss now, there is absolutely no guarantee whatsoever that we ever will get the chance to later.

I take this as a great lesson from my sister's life. There are many others, but this one hits home for me. I may not have everything I want in life, but who really does?

If Oprah is correct, then as long as I follow my bliss, the money will eventually follow. I guess we'll see. Either way, I'm in it for the long haul. After all, it's already bankrupted me, what else have I got to lose?

> *Take these chances*
> *Place them in a box until a quieter time*
> *Lights out, you up and die.*[9]

---

9   *"Ants Marching", Dave Matthews Band. © Bama Rags, Inc. and reproduced with permission. All rights reserved.*

Let's Call It a Postscript

Some time has passed since I finished the last chapter. I sent the book out to my publisher. The editor made notes and I made changes. It's now late November 2008 and the world has changed drastically. There are a few more experiences that I want to share and the publisher agreed to let me make additions.

First, about the script—the producer suddenly stopped responding to my e-mails. I was a bit frustrated, but I figured I'd let it go and just chalk it up to more Hollywood crap. I later found out from a writer/director friend, Reggie Blythewood, that the producer was no longer with the prodco. He had just vanished. Not sure what new company he'll pop up at or if he will at all, but I think I'll just turn that script into a book. That way, people can read what I write directly and if a prodco wants to turn it into a movie, we can talk about that. But at least I won't be on hold until they are ready.

So...

Times are hard across the country for everyone. Scores of banks have failed, including Lehman Brothers, and yesterday Citibank announced it was in trouble. Today the government promised to bail out the largest bank in the world. Gas went upwards of five dollars and has now come back down to two dollars per gallon. GM, Ford and Chrysler are on the verge of bankruptcy. The value of my family's home has dropped more than $400,000, and more people are in foreclosure than ever in history.

Things are at such a critical point that the nation looked past its normal prejudices and elected the first black President of the United States. So even though we're in horrible economic times, I'm proud of America. And I'm very proud of Barack Obama for the grace and dignity with which he faced all the nasty lies that were leveled against him during the campaign. I'm sure I would have snapped if I were he.

I worked hard to do my part from the beginning to help him get elected, from financial support to phone calls to swing states, but I must admit I don't know that I ever really believed he'd win. I knew he *should*. I just didn't believe he would. And the reality of his victory brings a major paradigm shift to my thinking. Anything truly is possible. Things can change.

Even Hollywood.

The book has taken much longer to finish than I expected and if it doesn't sell well, I'll probably need to find a new job, so I've been doing a few job interviews. A short while ago I interviewed with Aflac—yeah, the duck company.

The interview took place here in the Valley, in Sherman Oaks. As I waited for the elevator in the parking garage, business-suited up, a man approached dressed like a hip-hop Johnny Cash—black pants and boots, but with a kind of dragon design in the sequins of his black shirt, wearing six or so gold bracelets. Maybe they were real gold—maybe not.

A young lady who knew him from the building asked if he'd seen a cell phone she'd lost. He told her "no" as the elevator opened and we entered.

I press the button for the fourth floor. He was apparently going to the same place. Since the lady in the garage called him Richard, I wondered if he might be the same Richard I was to meet—you never know in L.A. He commented to me that it was a terrible thing to lose a cell phone. I agreed.

When we arrived on our floor, he asked where I was going. I told him 429. He said, "Oh, I thought you might have been coming to audition for me."

"Really? What are you guys casting?"

"It's a spinoff of *Ocean's Eleven*—called *Baby O*, really cool."

I wished him good luck and walked the opposite way down the hall. To my surprise, I had to about-face; I'd read the sign wrong. Aflac was right next door to the casting office.

I entered Aflac and waited. The Richard I was there to meet was in another interview and he was running late. I was bored. I looked around the cramped waiting area. There was barely room for two chairs and the giant stuffed Aflac duck next to me. In the corner behind the duck was a narrow trophy case full of awards for that office having sponsored golf tournaments. I thought that seemed odd.

It then occurred to me that *Ocean's Eleven* starred Julia Roberts. The thought of my experience with the receptionist who originally motivated me to write this book ran through my mind.

It also starred Brad Pitt. I started wondering whether Plan B, and thus Jeremy Kleiner, had anything to do with *Baby O*.

I noticed my shoes were dusty. I hadn't worn dress shoes since my sister's funeral. I had nothing to wipe them with. Then I thought about the plush white bottom of the giant stuffed Aflac duck next to me. As I entertained myself thinking how I could maneuver my feet below his plush white duff and get enough pressure for a good shine, I heard noises.

Actors began arriving in the hallway. I could see their shadows and hear them asking questions about headshots and sides.[10]

I started wondering why I was interviewing for an insurance job when I knew my heart wasn't in it. I started kicking myself, wondering why I hadn't been quick-witted enough to ask Richard, "Is there a part for someone like me in the film?" Maybe he was hinting that there was. I thought about crashing the audition. Actors do it all the time. Why not?

I figured I'd go into the hall, and if I saw anyone that even closely resembled my type, I'd crash the audition.

---

10 *Sides are the script pages actors use to audition.*

I asked the receptionist if there was a bathroom. As I'd hoped, it was down the hall. "Let me get you the key." She handed me a small, stuffed, plush Aflac duck with a key around its neck. I thought to myself—*Now this is perfect for polishing my shoes.*

I opened the door.

They weren't casting my type.

In the hallway were dozens of beautiful women and seven Asian guys. Crap! These women were striking—80% blonde, 100% busty, all in tight slutty miniskirts, all taller than 5'9", and all about twenty-five years old. Not the best audition for me to crash. I walked to the bathroom instead.

On my way I passed a young janitor whose eyes were bugging out of his skull as he snapped pictures of the actresses with his cell phone camera. He was grinning so intensely, and he was so focused, that he didn't notice me at all.

In the bathroom, I tried to figure out what to do with the duck while I relieved myself. It didn't fit easily into my suit pocket, but I managed.

After I washed my hands and removed the duck from my pocket, I remembered I wanted to polish my shoes. I knew already that this experience was going into this book, but what I didn't know when I pushed the duck's plush white duff onto my shoe leather was that it talked.

"AFLAC... AFLAC... AAAFFFLAAAC!!!!" the duck screamed, its now famous commercial lines, as I violated it against the top of my shoe. I laughed so hard, I couldn't quiet myself before exiting the bathroom.

In the hallway, more men had gathered from offices all over the building to get a gander at the ladies. The janitor was still snapping pictures and grinning.

I passed a new group of four more Asian guys, who really did look a lot alike—all with punk hairdos, sleeveless shirts and work boots. They did a smiling double take at me. It's L.A., so everyone smiles. I wondered if they'd thought I was someone else or had seen me on some forgotten commercial that finally started airing. I was the only one in the hallway in a suit and tie, so maybe they thought I was someone important.

As I approached the Aflac office, the casting office door swung open revealing a smiling 6-foot blonde, about twenty-five years old, with huge breasts. Surprisingly, she stepped back into the office to make room for me to enter. I glanced in and saw about twenty more blondes before I pointed to the Aflac door and thanked her.

I looked back down the hall as she exited. Sixty or eighty people, all just alike, all with the same appointment time, all smiling. At least there was parking in the building, and at least it was a real movie. I wondered how many roles there were to cast.

The point of this little observation is this—such scenes only happen in Hollywood. It's a town of dreams and dreamers. As I continued waiting for my interview, I couldn't help fantasizing about being in *Baby O* with Julia Roberts, George Clooney, Don Cheadle and Brad Pitt. I thought about sharing my Jeremy Kleiner story and other observations with them, and about listening to them hold forth on their perspectives on Hollywood.

But until then, I had to wait in the tiny space, next to the giant, stuffed, famous duck, whose commercials had aired much more often than mine. This is Hollywood after all, and that duck has what I want—and what each person in that hallway wants: life in front of the Hollywood sign.

I guess under those circumstances, it makes sense that the duck would be offended that I used it to polish my shoes. After all, he's already a star, and stars don't polish shoes.

—T.R. Locke, Burbank, CA

Acknowledgements

There are so many people to thank that I'm most afraid of forgetting someone. I hope I don't.

Along with God, I want to thank first, my wife, Lisa, and daughter, Aja, who have supported and journeyed with me throughout my various incarnations of insanity. You are the stars that guide me in the darkness. I would be lost without you. I love you dearly.

To everyone at Media City and Wish I Knew® Books, thanks for taking a chance on me; I hope it pays off, too. My editor, Jill Rembar—wow—and I thought it was a clean manuscript. I see why they gave you an Emmy. Thank you so much. Jana Rade at Impact Studios, for a great cover and book design—absolutely fantastic.

My writing group, Wayne, Cat, Karen, David, and Vivian for all your patient feedback, not only on this book, but through many scripts in the past and more to come in the future.

The fam: Mom, Pops, James, Cherry, Chris, Rita, Selena, Mahonna, Aaron, Rachel, Jaime, Theo, Aaron II, Melzada, Norma, Richard, Patrick, Tiffany, Michael, Camille, Mike Jr., Pop Peter, Deborah, Peter Jr., Brian, Jermel and Lala. Thanks for the encouragement and understanding.

To my boys, Henry, Nate, Byron, PCH, Darryl, Josh, Blackwell, Muay Thai Dave, Darnell, Evans, Mike, Dwayne, Mel, Robert, PRH, and Kenny. To my girls, Angie, Luann, Annet, PDH, Lisa H., Mom H. Keep your fingers crossed.

To my interviewees, for their amazing openness and honesty, thank you. I am in your debt.

To Barack and Michelle Obama, and everyone who made history voting Obama '08. Wow.

Most of all, thanks to each of you for reading my book. I appreciate you and I wish you courage and success in whatever bliss you pursue. ~TRL

If you enjoyed reading this book, please go to www.amazon.com (or your favorite book web site) and post a review. Also, remember to tell friends, family and co-workers about it (or blog about it, note it on Facebook, MySpace, etc.). Your positive comments help encourage new authors and strengthen the power of the people over corporations. Thank you.

If you have ideas for other Wish I Knew® books or experiences you'd like to see shared in future editions of "What I Wish I Knew® Before I Moved to Hollywood," please e-mail wishiknewbooks@gmail.com. Please include your name and phone contact information unless you wish to remain anonymous. (To include information from an anonymous source, Wish I Knew® Books must be able to verify validity.) However, we are very interested in hearing your stories either way and invite you to share them with us.

If you would like to be on our e-mail list—list members receive info on future releases, have opportunities to participate in Wish I Knew® surveys for future books, get discounts and free offers on books and more—please send an e-mail to the address above with the word "List" in the subject line. Wish I Knew® Books will never share or sell your private information or e-mail address.

Thank you,

Wish I Knew® Books

Keep an eye out for future Wish I Knew® Books including:

"I Do? —What I Wish I Knew® Before I Got Married"
(Coming Spring/Summer 2009)

LaVergne, TN USA
25 January 2010
171104LV00002B/45/P

9 780981 898308